Evil Bitches

Beth Mitchell

Published by Trellis Publishing, 2021.

While every precaution has been taken in the preparation of this book, the publisher assumes no responsibility for errors or omissions, or for damages resulting from the use of the information contained herein.

EVIL BITCHES

First edition. July 10, 2021.

Copyright © 2021 Beth Mitchell.

ISBN: 979-8223919155

Written by Beth Mitchell.

EVIL BITCHES

BETH MITCHELL

Judith and Alvin Neelley are an American married couple who were convicted of two torture murders in the early 1980s in Georgia and Alabama. Judith became the youngest woman to ever be sentenced to death in the United States; however, the Alabama governor at the time commuted her death penalty to life imprisonment in 1999; likely due to her age. Alvin died in prison in 2005 at the age of 52 due to complications resulting from surgery. Unlike most murderous couples, Judith was the primary antagonist in this relationship with much speculation that her higher IQ and deep-seated hatred of herself and others led to her actions.

Early Lives

Alvin Neelley

Alvin Howard Neelley was born on 15 July 1953 in Trion, Georgia; a heavily-wooded small village in the northwest corner of the state. The youngest of three children, his older brother and sister were enamored of Alvin and they all played well together. His childhood was a happy one, full of laughter and games, and of many friends from among the neighborhood children. He swam in creeks, fished, hunted, and became a boy scout. Alvin would continue to live this charmed life until he reached adulthood.

Alvin attended Fort McHenry Elementary School and from the get-go he was the class clown who loved to tell jokes and tease his teachers. He was well-liked and popular; however, he particularly enjoyed teasing the girls, oftentimes collecting frogs with which to scare them.

By the fifth grade, Alvin started to test the proverbial waters with authorities. One time he misbehaved by standing at the classroom window and was promptly spanked by a teacher and another time he talked back to the principal which also got him into trouble.

In seventh grade Alvin started taking girls to the pool—a pool in which the owner let him attend for free because of the paying crowd he would attract. In fact, he always attracted a large admiring crowd.

When he became a teenager, Alvin turned to crime and became a car thief.

Judith Ann Neelley

Judith Ann Adams was born on 7 June 1964 in Murfreesboro, Tennessee, approximately 90 miles south of Nashville. At the time, Murfreesboro was "a dingy little town of seedy trailer parks and honkey-tonks." Judith's mother was a housewife and her father was a construction worker and carpenter; the latter of whom she rarely saw, much to her disappointment. She also had an older sister named Dottie, an older brother named James, who everyone called Jimbo, and younger brothers, Davey and Bill. The Adams' lived in the Walter Hill section of Murfreesboro and despite not being affluent, they were not poor either, and Judith would never claim to have been deprived of anything.

Judith attended the Walter Hill School during the day and then played with friends until dinnertime. When her father started his own construction company in 1973, his income increased but he remained rather distant from his daughter, particularly when he would drink. For Christmas that same year her father gave her a blonde doll with a pink polka-dot body named Drowsey that talked when its cord was pulled, as well as a "Tote-A-Tune" small red keyboard with a carrying strap and book of songs. Over the years these two toys would become her most beloved possessions.

One Saturday evening in March 1974 when Judith was nine years of age, her father got atop his motorcycle, intoxicated, and subsequently slammed into the highway guardrail, killing himself. While she had always been the quiet child, her father's death turned her into stone.

In the fall of 1979 26-year-old Alvin Neelley fell head over heels in love with 15-year-old Judith Ann Adams, and vice versa. The two eloped very quickly after meeting and embarked upon a joint life of crime.

Crimes

On 11 September 1982, Rome, Georgia, Youth Development Center employee Ken Dooley's house was shot at four times. Prior to the incident he received a telephone call from an unidentified woman later discovered to have been Judith who stated that the attack was a direct result of her being sexually abused while incarcerated at the Youth Development Center. The following day fellow employee Linda Adair's home was firebombed with a Molotov cocktail after she received a similar telephone call. The unidentified female caller said that both Dooley and Adair would die for the abuse she endured in the Youth Development Center in Rome.

Soon thereafter the couple took up armed robbery. Once, Judith was arrested for robbing a woman in a parking lot at gunpoint in Georgia while she was nine months pregnant with twins. After giving birth in jail, temporary custody of the children was awarded to Alvin's parents until she was released.

Lisa Millican

Lisa Ann Millican was a 13-year-old girl who was abducted by Judith and Alvin and subsequently raped, beaten, tortured, and killed.

Born in 1969, Millican had suffered sexual abuse by her father since the age of ten and had been removed from her family's home in Lafayette, Georgia, a little more than a month before she was murdered. She was placed into a home in Rome before being transferred to the Ethel Harpst Home in Cedartown. She was housed in a facility not because she was a delinquent but because she had been living in her mother's car with her other siblings—in poverty—and had nowhere else to go.

She persuaded the house parent at Harpst Home to take her and a group of her friends to the Riverbend Mall on the night of 25 September 1982. Judith picked up Millican at the mall. At trial it was brought out that the Neelleys searched the streets of Rome looking for a young girl for Alvin and that they had planned to inject the victim with drain cleaner to kill her.

Judith drove them to a hotel in Franklin, Georgia, where Millican was forced to have sex with Alvin before being handcuffed and made to sleep naked on the floor.

The following morning the Neelleys picked up their two-year-old twins and drove to Scottsboro, Alabama, where they stayed in room 12 at the Five Points Motel. There, Judith repeatedly beat Millican with a stick but as she was not rendered unconscious Millican was brutally raped by Alvin later that day and the following morning. Millican was handcuffed and forced to stay in the bathroom while at the hotel and was subjected to repeated rapes by Alvin.

The next day they left Scottsboro with Millican handcuffed inside Judith's car. They followed highway 35 from Scottsboro to Fort Payne and then to Rocky Glade at the edge of Little River Canyon where they parked along the rim. Judith testified that she took Millican to the base of a nearby tree and told her to lie face down on the ground. Judith removed a syringe from her purse and, after telling Millican that the injection would put her to sleep so that Judith could leave without Millican knowing where she went, injected her in the neck with Liquid Drano because she had heard that this was a quick and undetectable way to kill someone. Unfortunately for Millican, the drain cleaner didn't do what Judith thought it would. Despite complaining about the pain, Millican didn't die. The subsequent five injections—into her neck, arms, and buttocks—also failed to kill her. Millican was subjected to this torture for at least 30 minutes. After repeatedly begging for her life, Judith told Millican to walk to the edge of the canyon and stand with her back to Judith. Then Judith shot her. Instead of falling into the canyon as Judith had planned she fell backward along the edge of the canyon, lying face-up and bleeding. Judith used her knee to push Lisa off the cliff and into the canyon. She then tossed the towel-wrapped syringes into the canyon along with her bloodied jeans. Judith's children slept through the entire thing.

Millican's body had landed on the floor of Little River Canyon, a densely wooded area most people used as a garbage dump and 80 feet below the precipice from where Judith had pushed her lifeless body.

On the evening of 29 September 1982 DeKalb County Sheriff's Office received a call from a woman who gave detailed directions to "a young girl's body." That night, Deputy James Mays and other deputies found Millican's body, shot to death, bearing puncture wounds from the hypodermic needles, and crumpled over a fallen tree. The next morning her body was removed from the canyon with a rope. Investigators also found three empty syringes and a pair of bloodied jeans near where Millican's body was found and were unsure as to whether this evidence had anything to do with Millican's death as there was much debris around the crime scene. The Alabama Department of Forensic Science in Huntsville ascertained that the blood on the jeans did, in fact, belong to Millican; however, they were too large to have been hers. At trial Judith stated that they were hers and because Millican didn't fall off the cliff when she was shot, Judith's pushing her with her knee caused her jeans to become bloodstained. They also discovered that the syringes contained drain cleaner.

Had Judith not informed authorities about Millican's fate or where her body was buried, the DeKalb County Sheriff's Office might not have discovered it for years because Millican was from Rome, Georgia, like the Neelleys, so the search for her body was focused there. The entire investigation was subsequently focused in Rome, Georgia, because that's where Millican was from and where she had disappeared. Detective Kenneth Kines was assigned the case and discovered Millican's sad childhood of sexual abuse, removal from her home, placement in the Open Door Home in Rome for 30 days, and assignment and removal in four different foster homes before being relocated to the Harpst Home. She was described as sexually precocious and unpopular with the other girls with whom she lived. One on occasion, Millican had kicked another girl in the stomach hard enough to cause a miscarriage. However, despite her poor behavior, Kines did not find any enemies or motives for her death.

When Judith called to inform police about the location of Millican's body she had said, "Y'all looking for Lisa Ann Millican on run from the Harpst Home?" This puzzled investigators and especially Mike Jones of the Walker County Department of Family and Children Services who had handled Millican's original case in Lafayette. He stated that the term "on run" was not how most people referred to runaways but that it was an insider's expression and quite common among those who had served time in the juvenile justice system. This hint enabled police to focus upon someone who likely had a juvenile record and some type of placement at the Youth Detention Center or similar facility.

When the taped recording of Judith's telephone call was played for 13-year-old Debbie Smith—a local girl who had been approached by a woman in a brown car on 4 October and was offered a ride—she identified the voice on the tape as the same as the woman who approached her. Later that evening—4 October—the Neelleys abducted their next victims: John Hancock and Janice Kay Chatman.

Even more damning for Judith was Hancock who, upon hearing the tape, exclaimed, "That's the damn woman that shot me!" in front of police.

John Hancock and Janice Kay Chatman

Upon first meeting the Neelleys, Judith identified herself to John Hancock and his fiancée Janice Kay Chatman as "Lady Sundown." They got into her brown Dodge and eventually met up with Judith's husband, Nightrider, on a dirt road north of Rome. Hancock testified that Nightrider drove a red vehicle and had two children in the car with him. Hancock was instructed to ride with Alvin while Janice stayed in

Judith's vehicle. Whereas Hancock said he felt a bit apprehensive he did not feel overtly threatened at that time.

They drove around in the vehicles for a while; into Alabama and back to Georgia. When they stopped again so Hancock could relieve himself, Judith told him to walk down the road away from the vehicles and this was where Judith shot him in the back. He stayed on the ground, playing dead, until he was sure that both vehicles left before running to find help.

Arrest and Investigation

Upon finding out about the anonymous phone call regarding Millican's body, Floyd County Sheriff's Department's Bill Whitner sought out Kines to discuss with him his own case of an unidentified female caller who informed him about a shooting and a firebombing months earlier. Puzzle pieces were connected and investigators began looking at former female Youth Development Center detainees for a suspect.

After Hancock told Kines that the vehicles driven by those who had abducted him and his fiancée bore out of state license plates, Kines asked juvenile officer Elaine Snow for a list of girls who had been placed in the Youth Development Center who were from out of state. The list contained 25 names.

After a thorough investigation one name was left—Judith Ann Neelley. Whereas Hancock said that the picture did resemble the woman who shot him he couldn't be sure; however, Debbie Smith identified Judith immediately as the woman who tried to pick her up. Before he was able to locate Judith, Kines had found that she had already been arrested at a motel in Murfreesboro on 9 October 1982 for passing bad checks. When no sign of Chatman was to be found, Kines was sure that she was dead.

Alvin was arrested a few days later.

Alvin asked for a lawyer, waived his right to remain silent and provided a lengthy and detailed statement about the Millican case that implicated his wife as the criminally-deviant mastermind of whom he was afraid and who planned the abductions, rapes, tortures, and murders, as well as the earlier shooting and firebombing; that she had forced him to rape Millican and Chatman; and that she murdered the two women. He drew a map detailing where Chatman's body could be find.

In another interrogation room down the hall Judith waived her right to an attorney and also answered questions. First, she said that Adair had forced her to have sex with Dooley at the Youth Development Center and that she was a victim of a prostitution ring operated from the facility; both allegations were later proven untrue. Judith then provided chilling detail about the final days of Millican's and Chatman's lives.

Judith stated that she saw Millican in a video arcade at the Riverbend Mall and that she had noticed the young girl because she looked like Joanie Cunningham from the popular television show *Happy Days*. Allegedly, Millican had left with Judith willingly because she did not want to return to Harpst Home. For a couple of days they drove around in Judith's vehicle with her twin children in the back seat during the day and stayed in motels at night in which Millican was handcuffed to the bed and forced to sleep, naked, on the floor. Judith said that instead of letting Millican return and say what had happened to her it would be better to kill the young woman.

Chatman's body was found precisely where Alvin said it was; on a back road in Chattooga County, Georgia.

Authorities then executed a search warrant at Judith's mother's—Barbara Adams—house in Murfreesboro as that was where the Neelleys had been staying. Among the evidence collected there were handcuffs, knives, guns, and two CB radios the two used to communicate with each other while hunting for prey using the handles "Lady Sundown" and "Nightrider."

Trial and Sentence

Judith's trial began on 7 March 1983, a few months after giving birth to a third child while she was incarcerated. Her appointed public defender was Bob French who said that after his first meeting with Judith he disliked her immensely.

The first course of action he undertook was to seek youthful offender status for her since she under 21 years of age so as to transfer her case to juvenile court; however, Judge Randall Cole denied his motion. French then asked for a psychological assessment to determine Judith's fitness for trial. These assessments were done in January 1983 and it was determined that she was fit for trial, of superior intelligence, and possessed no delusional or suicidal ideations or tendencies.

During the voir dire jury selection process, French sought to find jurors who would likely sympathize with Judith as a victim of Alvin's alleged barbarism who controlled her throughout their entire relationship and crime spree as evidenced by questions as to men's sensitivity to women's emotional problems and the traditional role of a male head of household.

French also tried to get Judith "cleaned up" a bit for court. She had dental work done by Dr. Steven Brewer and French purchased some clothing for her at the upscale Black's Department Store for her trial appearances.

French's primary course of action was to portray Judith as an unwilling victim to Alvin's murderous rampage. He told the jury in his opening statement that Judith had fallen for Alvin at the age of 15 (which was true) but that soon thereafter he subjected her to savage beatings and forced her to feed and bathe him. French added that Judith was controlled sexually by Alvin and, consequently, had become brainwashed.

Thus, throughout the Millican trial, Judith tried to portray herself as Alvin's reluctant victim during Millican's ordeal; however, investigators stated that there was no doubt that Judith was the mastermind throughout their crime spree. At one point, while testifying about the abuse she allegedly suffered at her husband's hands, Judith dropped her head and, with her hair draped over her face, appeared to cry. DeKalb County prosecutor Richard Igou told Judith to raise her head and everyone in the courtroom noticed that she was completely dry-eyed. He stated that Judith had an extreme coldness about her that was pure evil and had no remorse whatsoever for her actions.

Among the first witnesses for the prosecution were three young girls who Judith had tried to pick up. In addition to Smith who identified Judith's voice and image during the preliminary investigation, Suzanne Clonts identified Judith as the woman who had asked if she was alone at Aladdin's Castle arcade at the Riverbend Mall on 25 September—the day Millican disappeared—as well as Diane Bobo who was also approached by Judith and asked to go for a ride on 3 October. None of these witnesses testified that they saw Alvin in the vicinity or that Judith appeared to be beaten or otherwise abused.

The next witness was Hancock who Judith had shot after abducting him and his fiancée Chatman. Igou attempted to emphasize that it was Judith alone who had abducted them and shot him. However, French got Hancock to admit that Alvin was the first to contact her on the CB radio, decided where they would meet, and chastised her for taking too long in shooting Hancock; thus giving the jury potential cause to believe that Alvin might, in fact, have been in control of the situation. On redirect, Igou quickly reestablished Judith's role as instigator and mastermind of the situation.

For the defense, French called Jo Ann Browning—Alvin's first wife—to the stand. They had been married for three years during the mid-19070's and was the mother to three of their children. Browning testified that he had beaten her during the entire course of their marriage, even during her pregnancies, and that Alvin had drugged and attempted to rape her teenage sister. She also testified that when she had tried to leave him on several occasions he threatened their children and she was only able to escape when he met and fell for Judith. On cross-examination Igou damaged her credibility by proving that she had already remarried before she and Alvin had divorced thus making her a bigamist and was also a liar. Despite her claims of ongoing abuse neither had Browning suffered a broken bone nor were any of their children damaged by his alleged beatings. When Browning left the witness stand she was noticeably upset and angry.

French then called Judith to the stand who immediately dispelled any preconceived image that she was a passive victim. She joked with her attorney during questioning and laughed easily which prompted French to ask her how she deals with stress, fear, or nervousness to which she replied by smiling a lot.

She said that she had left her unstable home willingly with Alvin and that he was an "ardent and romantic suitor." However, Judith testified that Alvin's sexual advances were crude, selfish, and became increasingly violent and, as a result, she became his sex slave. She testified that she bathed and dressed him and while he was employed at a convenience store she was the one who did his menial tasks of sweeping, mopping, and stocking. She said that she cooked for and fed him and that if she did anything wrong he would beat her. He allegedly taught her robbery and forgery and his intense jealousy affected their relationship even though she said that she had always been faithful to him. She further testified that her false allegations of sexual abuse at the Youth Development Center were of Alvin's making, and as she continued her testimony about beatings and rapes her role as a victim was becoming more believable.

Judith testified that on the day of Millican's abduction Alvin had told her that he wanted a virgin. She stated that her part in the beating was at his behest and that she witnessed Alvin's multiple rapes of Millican—as did their children. Judith testified that he had been alongside her during Millican's torture and death, giving her instructions the entire time, and that after Millican was dead Alvin masturbated. She said that he forced her to make the phone calls to the Rome and Fort Payne police. She accused Alvin of forcing her to abduct Hancock and Chatman and to murder Chatman, and that she had just abducted another girl for Alvin in Murfreesboro when she was arrested.

Igou knew that Judith was putting on a show because he saw the real cold and heartless woman who was initially brought into custody and was amazed that someone so young could be so depraved and indifferent. He attacked French's methodical defense strategy by pointing out that amidst all of Alvin's beatings Judith only suffered two broken fingers and a chipped tooth; hardly the injuries a woman who was regularly beaten would have sustained.

With respect to Chatman's death, Judith testified that Alvin gave the initial order to shoot her but because Chatman was screaming Judith shot her two more times and Igou succeeded in getting Judith to admit that she did that of her own accord.

Igou presented several photographs of Alvin and Judith posing with various guns and family members and in every single one of them she was smiling rather happily. Judith testified that Alvin arranged all of the photos and had ordered her to smile in that way. In essence, Judith attempted to persuade the jury that the only things she had control of in her life involved eating and going to the bathroom. Everything else, she said, was dictated by her husband.

The prosecution also called Dr. Alexander Salillas from the Alabama Department of Mental Health as a rebuttal witness who testified that Judith did, in fact, know the difference between right and wrong at the time of the crimes and had made a deliberate and conscious decision to kill Millican and Chatman. When asked about some small bruises Judith had in one of the pictures, Igou asked Dr. Salillas whether they could be the result of a beating to which Salillas answered in the negative. He said that the bruising was likely a result of playful pinching. Needless to say, his testimony seriously damaged Judith's credibility. Dr. Salillas was the last witness to testify.

Igou's closing argument was short and to the point, reiterating that Judith did not suffer abuse at Alvin's hands because of the lack of physical scars and that Judith had not been brainwashed but she, herself, planned, executed, and enjoyed her crimes, and that she was evil. On the other hand, French's closing argument took over two hours and made odd references to the Bible, to the Chinese principle of yin and yang, and to George du Maurier's character of Svengali in *Trilby*. French also asked the jury to live according to their Christianity and to permit their "feminine side" and "love side" to help find Judith not guilty. He read some of Alvin's letters to Judith while they were incarcerated. He also oddly mentioned snakes, insects, and birds and the female multi-orgasmic response. Throughout all of his lengthy and bizarre closing argument French made sure that he reminded the jury on several occasions to hold Judith to the standard of a woman who was savagely and severely beaten by her husband every single day of her life.

On 21 March at 4:30 p.m. Judge Cole gave the jury its instructions and by 10:45 a.m. the following day they had reached their verdict: guilty of kidnapping and homicide. Sentencing arguments by the prosecution and defense followed and later that night the jury had decided by a 10-2 vote that Judith be sentenced to life in prison. In Alabama, this decision only serves to inform the judge of the jury's opinion with the final decision resting with the judge him- or herself. After a sentencing hearing on 18 April, Judge Cole sentenced the 18-year-old Judith Ann Neelley to die in the electric chair.

Following her conviction for the murder of Lisa Ann Millican, to avoid another death sentence Judith pled guilty to the kidnapping and attempted murder of John Hancock and the kidnapping and murder of Janice Chatman. Alvin, not wanting to be slandered by Judith in another trial, pled guilty to kidnapping with bodily harm and intent to murder and was given two life terms. He died in prison in 2005 as a result of complications sustained during surgery.

Judith was sent to death row at Julia Tutwiler Prison for Women in Wetumpka, Alabama. After her sentence was commuted to life she was transferred to a woman's prison in Louisiana on an interstate compact as she remains the prisoner of the state of Alabama.

Alvin later told law enforcement officers that he and Judith had knowledge of other women's murders in Georgia and Alabama; however, the murderous couple was not linked to any others.

Aftermath

In August 1984 a young woman named Casey told Murfreesboro police that she had been abducted a few years prior and had come across Judith's picture in the newspaper, thus identifying her as her abductor. Casey said that Judith had talked to her all night, bragging about her crimes and saying that she had killed a few girls and throughout this entire time Judith never appeared nervous or afraid. Judith allegedly told her that she enjoyed the look on people's faces when she pulled a gun on them. Casey was the last person Judith had picked up before being arrested. While Judith was being arrested Alvin was holding Casey at gunpoint in the bathroom and when police had taken Judith away, he let her go.

In 1994 a woman shot herself to death at a home in Etowah County, Alabama, allegedly due to a suicide pact she and Judith had made. There were telephone recordings between the woman and Judith detailing their plans and how they wanted their bodies disposed of after the fact. When investigators contacted the prison to alert them the warden found Judith in her death-row cell with her wrists slashed by a disposable razor; however, the wounds were not deep enough to constitute a serious suicide attempt.

Judith appealed for a new trial that was denied in March 1987. The United States Supreme Court denied her final appeal in 1988 and affirmed her death sentence in 1989. It appeared very likely that

Judith would be the first woman executed in Alabama in over 40 years; however, then-Governor Fob James commuted her death sentence to life on 15 January 1999. At this time there was much speculation that she would eventually be eligible for parole, with some reports placing this date as early as 2014 because according to Alabama law at that time, anyone convicted to life in prison was automatically eligible for parole after 15 years.

Of particular interest was that the day James commuted her sentence was the same day in which the state had requested a date for her execution. This was amidst the whole Karla Faye Tucker death penalty case and the backlash by Christian fundamentalists over Tucker's alleged conversion to Christianity which they argued should be grounds for commuting her death sentence. Judith attempted the same tactic and many speculate that since James himself was a Christian fundamentalist he sought to demonstrate his beliefs by commuting Judith's death sentence to life. James' reasons for commuting her sentence was that the original jury had made the recommendation that she be sentenced to life in prison yet the trial judge sentenced her to death and that killing her would not be in the best interests of justice. He was succeeded by Don Siegelman three days later.

Ninth Circuit District Attorney Mike O'Dell—who was an assistant district attorney in 1983 and helped prosecute Judith's case—stated that he was "shocked and disturbed" upon finding out about James' commutation and, shortly thereafter, spearheaded efforts to change state law to ensure that Judith remained behind bars for the rest of her life.

Following hearings by the Alabama House and Senate Judiciary Committees, in 2003 the state legislature enacted legislation that mandated that any death sentence commutation automatically became a sentence of life without the possibility of parole and this law was made retroactive to September 1998 to ensure that Judith Neelley would remain incarcerated for the rest of her life.

On 28 February 2008 the Neelleys' case was profiled on Investigation Discovery's *Most Evil*. On a scale developed by Michael Stone, a forensic psychiatrist, Judith was ranked a category 22 murderer; the "most evil" level for serial torture killers. On 23 October 2008, the Neelleys were profiled on *Wicked Attraction* in the episode entitled "Hearts of Darkness" in 2011 Judith was featured on *Deadly Women*.

PSYCHO GIRL : THE TRUE STORY OF CATHERINE BIRNIE

JENA DICKENS

Catherine Margaret Harrison was born on May 23rd, 1951. Her partner, David John Birnie, was born on February 16th, 1951 and died on October 7th, 2015 by way of suicide. The duo was famously known throughout Australia as: The Killer Couple. They were from Perth, Australia and were found to have murdered four women ranging in age from 15 to 31 years old, over a span of about five weeks. Their fifth victim managed to escape through the bedroom window, while Catherine was distracted by a knock at the front door. The woman immediately ran and found help. The press referred to the heinous murders as the Moorhouse Murders. The victims were taken to Catherine and David's home located at 3 Moorhouse Street in Willagee, in Western Australia, a suburb of Perth.

Catherine was only two years old when her mother died in childbirth while giving birth to Catherine's younger brother. Her brother also died, two days later. Catherine's father, Harold, couldn't manage raising Catherine on his own at that time so she went to live with her maternal grandparents. When she was ten years old, Harold petitioned the court to receive custody of Catherine again, and he won. There always seemed to be a battle. Catherine's father didn't want her, but then wanted her, always back and forth. After Catherine was convicted of four counts of murder, it caused her father to suffer a nervous breakdown.

When Catherine was twelve years old she met a boy named David Birnie and they began dating two years later when they became teenagers. Both Catherine and David came from dysfunctional families. Their home life was chaotic and messy, literally as well as figuratively. David's mother was an alcoholic and his father was away at work the majority of the time. His father died in 1986 after battling a long illness. The house, as well as his mother, were messy and unkempt. She left her older children in charge of taking care of their younger siblings. She refused to do anything when it concerned the children and their welfare. Allegedly, David's mother would leave the refrigerator door open so that the children could eat throughout the day. David was the oldest of five children. David's school friends, as well as the local priest, deemed the family dysfunctional. The parents never prepared meals for their children, the house was always a mess, and the Priest, before marrying David's parents, said that he felt that their marriage would never lead to anything good. Little did he know how accurate his assumptions would be.

Catherine and David met through mutual friends shortly after David's family moved to the same Perth neighborhood as Catherine and her father. Catherine's father felt that David was trouble and a bad influence. Catherine had begun getting into a lot of trouble with the local police ever since the two of them met. Harold begged and pleaded with Catherine to stay away from David and stay out of trouble. Of course, this just brought the two closer. Whenever two kids are told not to do something, they go out of their way to blatantly disobey.

Even in adolescence David began exhibiting violent and perverse behavior. When David turned fifteen he dropped out of school and began working as jockey apprentice for Eric Parnham at the Ascot Race Course. While there, David would hurt the horses and also began his perverse career as an exhibitionist. David committed his first rape shortly after. By this point he had spent time in and out of jail for several charges ranging from misdemeanors to felonies. He built up a reputation around town as a sex and pornography addict.

Catherine was an accessory to a lot of crimes because of her involvement with David. They built up an extensive history of numerous charges including: breaking and entering, trespassing, unlawfully driving a motor vehicle, and theft. Catherine took the time, while in jail, to decide it was time to get away from David and start over. David had to serve a long jail sentence, while Catherine got off with probation. With the help of her parole officer, she found a job as a housekeeper working for the McLaughlin family. She ended up marrying the families' oldest son, Donald McLaughlin, on her twenty first birthday. They went on to have seven children. One of her children, however, was killed in a car accident while he was only an infant, leaving her with six of her children to take care of. Catherine was never really interested in motherhood though, and wasn't proud of her children and her family like another mother might be. She wasn't concerned about the children or keeping up with the house. Catherine was never truly happy. Her thoughts kept going back to her childhood love, David Birnie. The family that she had left never saw Catherine as a violent or evil person. Not unless she was around David.

Catherine finally reconnected with David Birnie after a thirteen year separation, four weeks after she gave birth to their seventh child. David had escaped from prison and the two of them had begun seeing each other. Catherine left her family and everything behind when David popped back into her life. They finally moved in together and Catherine had her last name changed to Birnie, although the couple never formally or legally got married. They moved into a white brick, two bedroom bungalow on Moorhouse Street. The house was unkempt, the property looked untended, and the house needed a fresh coat of paint. Catherine was completely dependent on David, emotionally and physically. Catherine was easily controlled and manipulated by David, and she would do anything and everything to make him happy. She never wanted to disappoint him. David had an insatiable sexual appetite and was said to have sex up to six times a day. He also accrued an extensive pornography collection and his brother claimed he always had someone. He always had a woman around. David's brother, James, had ended up staying with Catherine and David for a short while. James had just recently been released from prison after serving time for his own sex related offenses. He stayed with the couple for about six months. His brother went on to describe the numbing spray that David would spray on his penis before he had sex with all of the different women.

David and Catherine had exhausted all of their options sexually and began looking for new ways to pleasure themselves. They had spoken about abduction and rape, but had not realized that it would be just a few short weeks before they turned their fantasies into a heinous and perverted reality. Being as emotionally dependent on David as she was, it was easy for David to talk her into his abduction and rape plans. Catherine could never tell him no. She felt that she couldn't survive without him and would do anything to keep him. Catherine was completely codependent and David always seemed to be in control. She wanted David to have all the pleasure and excitement that he wanted but knew that they had exhausted all efforts between just the two of them.

The abductions, rapes, and brutal murders began on October 6th, 1986. The couple didn't really care who their victims were, as long as they were female and alone. Twenty two year old Mary Neilson arrived at the Moorhouse Street residence to inquire about some tires that David had for sale. Mary was a student at the University of Western Australia where she was pursuing her degree in Psychology. Once inside the house, David took Mary by knife point and chained her to their bed and gagged her. Catherine stood in the room and watched as David raped the girl repeatedly. After the rape, the couple took Mary to Gleneagles National Park. David raped her one more time and then strangled her with a nylon cord and stabbed her through the heart. The couple then buried Mary in a shallow grave. Catherine looked on while David committed these violent acts, however, she did not yet participate.

The second murder took place on October 20th. The victim was fifteen year old, Susannah Candy. Susannah was a high school student attending Hollywood High School. She lived with her parents and had two brothers and one sister. Catherine and David Birnie had been driving around for several hours that night in search of their next victim. The couple finally found a girl walking along Stirling Highway, by herself, trying to hitch a ride. As soon as she got into David's car she had a knife to her throat and she was taken to the Birnies' home. While at the home, she was forced to write letters to her family explaining that she decided to run away. David repeatedly raped Susannah while she lay bound and gagged. Catherine had gotten into the bed with them and tried to strangle her with the nylon cord, but Susannah began fighting back. They forced sleeping pills down her throat, and once she passed out they successfully strangled her with the cord. The couple took Susannah to the State Park and buried her in a shallow grave, like their previous victims. This was the first time that Catherine took part in the murder. Catherine never showed any form of remorse over what she had done. When later asked why she contributed she said,

"I wanted to see how strong I was within my inner self. I didn't feel a thing. It was like I expected. I was prepared to follow him to the end of the earth and do anything to see that his desires were satisfied. She was a female. Females hurt and destroy males."

On November 1st, the Killer Couple comes across their third victim, Noelene Patterson. Noelene was on her way home from work when her car ran out of gas. Noelene was a bar manager and had been working at Nedland's Golf Club that day. She was standing beside her car when David pulled up to her and offered his help. The thirty one year old got into David's car and was immediately met with a knife at her throat. She was taken to Moorhouse Street where she was bound and gagged, while being raped repeatedly. The original plan, like the others, was to kill the girl that same night. David had seemed to develop feelings for Noelene however. Catherine noticed the fondness that David had for the woman and became extremely jealous and increasingly upset. Noelene represented the type of person that Catherine could only wish to be and she absolutely despised her because of this. Catherine gave David an ultimatum at this point. She put the knife to her own chest and said, 'you either kill her tonight, or I will kill myself.' It was on the third night, after being given the ultimatum, that David gave Noelene several sleeping pills and then strangled her. She was then taken to the park and buried beside the other victims. Catherine admitted to taking pleasure in throwing sand in the victims face as David coldly buried her with no remorse.

Catherine and David's fourth victim, Denise Brown, suffered the same fate as the previous women who had the unfortunate experience of crossing paths with the Killer Couple. Denise Brown was twenty one years old, and was taken on November 5, 1986 while waiting at a bus stop. She was gagged and raped repeatedly before being put into the car and taken to Pine Plantation, where she was raped again while David waited for a blanket of darkness to fall. After it got dark he took her out and raped her again, while stabbing her in the neck. As David began burying her, thinking she was dead, Denise surprised the couple by sitting straight up in her grave. David struck her in the head twice with an axe as Catherine looked on in shock and amazement. David has said that he learned bodies would decompose at a faster rate if you stabbed them.

Detective Sergeant Paul Ferguson was the first to realize that he could be dealing with a serial killer, after the fourth woman was reported missing. Years later he recalled his experience while working on the case. He recalls how this case still haunts him and when asked why replied, "Because it was the most interesting and horrific I've had in my career," and "I have things tucked away back here that I pray to God I never pull out of the drawer." All of the missing women had come from relatively good homes and they never got into any real trouble. Their families found the phone calls and letters they received very suspicious.

The couples' fifth and final victim was seventeen year old Kate Moir. She was on her way home, after a night out with her friends, when she was abducted by the couple. The date of this final abduction was November 10th, 1986. Kate was the only one of their victims that was able to escape and run and find help. David had left the house for work that day. Catherine was home with Kate. She forced her to call her parents and tell them that she would be staying at a friend's house. When Catherine heard a knock at the door, she left Kate alone, untied, and went to see who was there. Kate took the opportunity to escape through the open window and ran half naked to the nearest store. She ran in crying and pleading for help. Kate was taken to the Palmyra police station and questioned. She was able to give the police a full description of Catherine and David, as well as inform the police of the couples' address. After their arrest, Catherine admitted to knowing Kate, but the couple said that the sexual acts were consensual and she was a willing participant. The police performed a search of the Birnie's home and found Kate's bag, as well as a pack of cigarettes that Kate had managed to hide in the ceiling in order to prove that she was there. After hours of questioning, Catherine and David finally admitted to the rape and murders of the four women and agreed to show the police where they had buried them. Three of the victims had been buried in Gleneagle State Forest and one on the Pine Plantation. The couple showed no emotion, whatsoever, as the police dug up the graves. David was the one who showed the police the locations of the women, except for one. Catherine insisted that she be the one to show them where Noelene was buried. She showed no regret, only anger. She spat on Noelene's grave and made her strong feelings of hate toward her very vocal to the detective. She explained to the police, in great detail, how much she despised Noelene Patterson. As they were leaving, David turned to Detective Katich and said chillingly, "What a pointless loss of young life." They showed absolutely no remorse for what they had done. This statement stuck with the detectives for years to follow. They couldn't believe how little the couple seemed to care or regret what they had been done. In some ways, however, they thought Catherine was relieved that it was finally over.

Catherine admitted to not caring about participating in the rapes and murders of the women, until they got to Denise Brown. "I think I must have come to a decision that sooner or later there had to be an end to the rampage. I had reached the stage when I didn't know what to do. I suppose I came to a decision that I was prepared to give her a chance." The brutal manner in which Denise was murdered seemed to hit Catherine hard. She witnessed David not only stab her repeatedly but strike her in the head with the axe. "Deep and dark in the back of my mind was yet another fear. I had a great fear that I would have to look at another killing like that of Denise Brown, the girl he murdered with the axe."

In response to Kate Moir's escape, due to Catherine's carelessness with her victim, she said, "I knew that it was a foregone conclusion that David would kill her, and probably do it that night. I was just fed up with the killings. I thought if something did not happen soon it would simply go on and on and never end."

Kate Moir survived the abduction and attacks of Australia's most infamous serial killers. Instead of remaining a victim, she chose to be a survivor. She also sought to seek reform for the way her government handled cases like hers.

"I want to see no parole for wilful murder. I want a reintroduction of wilful murder as a charge. I want truth in sentencing. I want no parole for sex offenders and child sex offenders. We have been softening our justice system for years."

Kate Moir is a married woman and mother of three children. She constantly fights for the changes and justice she deserves. The following are quotes that were made by Kate, again concerning Catherine's parole and the possibility of her release.

"I want the legacy that I leave to be that of a survivor and a hero, not a victim. But enough is enough."

"I want the Attorney General to change the law and stop reviewing Catherine Birnie's parole. She does not apply for it herself, it is automatically reviewed and every time it happens, it causes me incredible pain."

"Every time I hear that her parole is being reviewed, I relive the nightmare. It causes significant trauma because I relive it and it feels like it happened yesterday. My name was always protected because I was a minor at the time I was captured, but due to the internet, if anybody googles my name it is everywhere and linked to the Birnie killings."

The couple appeared in court on November 12th, 1986. This was just two days after their fifth victim had escaped and they were arrested. The court proceedings took place at Fremantle Magistrates Court. They both refused any kind of representation, no plea was entered, bail was refused, and they were remanded into custody. Catherine allegedly took photos and the couple also recorded video of their criminal acts. At trial, the police were in possession of the video evidence. On

February 10, 1987 a crowd gathered outside of the courthouse. When they saw the couple being ushered in for trial they screamed and chanted, "Hang the Bastards!" The community was outraged over the news of the serial killings that took place and wanted David and Catherine to receive the maximum sentence. They even wanted to reinstate the death penalty for David and Catherine Birnie.

Bill Power, the court reporter, spoke about the proceedings and the manners in which the couple acted while in court. He said that it would be something that would always stick with him, he would never forget.

"There was nothing distinctive about David and Catherine when they first appeared in court to face multiple murder charges in the serial killings which brought an end to the mystery of young women going missing off Perth streets."

"They were a rather nondescript, ordinary looking couple you might find running a petrol station in a country town. David was a weedy little man and Catherine his drab, slightly buxom wife with a very sour face. Both were accompanied by male police officers."

"If you have ever witnessed a wild cat go off, then try and imagine some hellcat in the confined spaces of a narrow staircase. Catherine Birnie fought against the guarding police officers and refused to allow any of them to touch her as she screamed and spat her words at them until she reached the dock and spotted her beloved, David. Only then did she calm down."

It had also been said previously, by some people in the community that the couple never looked like the type that could commit such violent acts. They looked like normal and ordinary people. But the secret horrors of what occurred in their home on Moorhouse Street would paint a very different image of the couple.

Trial Judge Justice Wallace said in trial, "Each of these horrible crimes were premeditated, planned, and carried out cruelly and relentlessly over a comparatively short period."

Right before Judge Wallace sentenced Catherine, he delivered the following message to her. He explained that he did not believe that even though she pled guilty, that she was truly sorry for what she had done. She had pled guilty and avoided a long trial, and spared the victims' families from having to relive over and over what happened to their loved ones, but she showed no remorse, no emotion, no sympathy for the crimes she had committed with David Birnie.

"You willingly joined in the selection of your unfortunate victims, carried them off at knifepoint, and held them in captivity for the sole purpose of the sexual gratification of your partner in crime and then murdered them, lest you be identified, and then finally mutilated them. You personally extinguished the life of two of your victims and certainly participated in the death of the third. The only appropriate punishment is the sentence I intend to impose, strict life security in prison."

Remember, Catherine was completely devoted, obsessed, and brainwashed when it came to David. She would do anything and everything for him to make sure he was happy. This is the driving factor that David used to manipulate and control her. He needed an accomplice and she was more than willing, and he knew it. Catherine and David received four separate life sentences for the abduction, torture, rape, and murder of Mary Neilson, Susannah Candy, Noelene Patterson, and Denise Brown. Under sentencing laws, their case was brought up every three years automatically for parole. Kate began a crusade to ensure that the couple remained in prison. She grew a social media presence and page entitled, We Support Kate, as well as worked with the Empowerment Foundation in an attempt to build an online reform petition. Kate also received support from Catherine's son, Peter. He chose not to release his surname to the public, due to the physical and emotional abuse he has been forced to face in relation to his mother's crimes. He had suffered personal and professional ruin, as soon as people learned about his family history. He had been turned down for jobs, lost jobs he had, and even lost his fiancé because of his family background. Peter was only five years old when his mother was arrested. He saw his mother on television because of it shortly after her arrest. When speaking out on the abuse he faced, he recalled horrible stories of what happened to him, and his siblings, while growing up. He also stated that the mandatory parole hearings, every three years, prevented him from getting on with his life. Having to hear about his mother and relive the violence his mother was responsible for every few years, was an interruption to his life, and it made it harder to maintain a sense of normalcy within his career life and personal life. In an interview with the West Australian, Peter stated, "I want the parole board to hear I don't want her out. I don't want to see her out." He also said, "I have had baseball bats to the head, I have been jumped on and kicked at. I have been knocked out."

After pleading guilty and receiving their sentences, David was initially sent to maximum security Fremantle Prison, he was eventually moved into solitary confinement. He did not get along with the other prisoners and was constantly getting into fights. The inmates frequently and violently attacked David. A day before he was due in trial for the charge of rape of an inmate, David hung himself in his jail cell. His suicide occurred in 2009 at Casuarina Prison. Catherine's request to attend David's funeral was refused.

Catherine was sent to Bandyup Women's prison where she was eventually employed as the head librarian. While in prison, the couple exchanged over 2600 letters, but were denied any other form of contact. Catherine's mandatory parole hearings were finally revoked in 2009, and her papers were subsequently marked: 'never to be released.'

While many people are against Catherine Birnie ever getting parole, one man stands against this argument. Perth QC Tom Percy disagrees with the opinion of people that had been saying that some people just don't deserve a second chance. The following quotes by Percy outline his argument of Catherine not remaining in prison and the likelihood of her harming the community, as well as his stance of being in favor of Catherine's parole.

"She should not be kept in prison to satisfy society's thirst for revenge."

"She has been there thirty odd years and you would think it might be time for us to say she has done her time. She has done her statutory minimum prescribed by the court, which was in possession of all of the facts."

"I am not sure she could really be a threat to anyone anymore, and all my information from Bandyup Womens' Prison is that she is a little old granny that goes about her work in the library like a church mouse."

"This case just so happened to be one that caught the public attention, even though she was not the prime mover in it. David is now dead."

"What's the point of keeping her in there? Sadly, it looks like she will never get parole, but I think she probably deserves it."

Despite his argument and fight to get Catherine released from prison, she still remains behind bars. She has not requested any new parole hearings, herself, as of yet. Some people in the community had gone as far as to say that if she were to be released, then maybe Percy should allow her to live with him in his residence.

It was now January of 1987. A letter written by Catherine Birnie, while in prison, eventually surfaced. It was a letter she had written to her six children in an attempt to explain some of her actions that led to her being placed in prison and why she left them in the first place. The letter reads as followed:

"Dear kids, Hi! Mum here...the reason I changed my name to Birnie was so that you kids wouldn't be hurt by the newspapers and television people. I am not proud of what has been said about me, but I have to live with that and the memories. As to why this happened, I can only hope that the doctors can help me to find out.....I never stopped loving any of you kids. Maybe I was wrong about leaving you but I thought you would be safer with your father."

Catherine's husband, Donald, claimed that he had still wanted her back. This was after trial and after he heard of the horrific acts she had committed with David. He stated, 'you can't stop loving someone after fifteen years of marriage.' Donald's mother stood firmly beside her son, saying that Catherine had been good and non-violent, until David cast his spell over her. Catherine's nephew, Leonard Nock, stood beside his aunt claiming, "All Aunt Cathy wanted was someone to lean on. She never had a mother. She is a very caring person. She and I are very close. I used to call her my mum. She was never the violent type, she never used to hit the kids. It is not the Cathy we used to know and love." In Catherine's letter she also persuaded the children to tell their father to divorce her. She said their father needed to move on and this was the way it needed to be done. She didn't hold out any hope for her eventual release and didn't want Donald to wait for her, because it was never going to happen. She also asked the children to get permission from Donald to write back to her, and maybe even one day go and visit her. The family put the entirety of the blame on David. They refused to admit to or believe that Catherine had anything to do with the violence. During their prison visits, the family also failed to even ask Catherine the question regarding her guilt or innocence. They didn't want to hear the answer, therefore, they never even asked the question.

Catherine Bernie was up for parole in 2013 and again in 2016. She was denied both years. She is once again up for review sometime in 2019. "Now barring any reason to keep her in, and revenge I don't consider enough of a reason. She should be released."-Percy

Despite Percy's statements, Catherine Birnie remains in prison to this very day, with little to no chance of parole. People, even to this day, wonder if the abductions, the perverse rape, and heinous murders would have continued long past the few weeks they had gotten away with it. If they had never been caught, would they have continued? Finally, were there other victims that they never confessed to? Other gravesites that have yet to be located? It is too late for David Birnie to tell anyone, but Catherine still has the chance to admit to any other wrongdoing she had done before her permanent home in prison forced her to keep distance between herself and her lover. I guess we will never know.

"I honestly believe that woman has never given those victims one ounce of consideration, both the dead victims and the families of the victims...They [David and Catherine Birnie] were parasites who lived off of each other. The most evil people I have ever, ever come across."-Detective Paul Ferguson.

CELESTE BEARD

CHRISTINE CHIP

"She is really in my mind, a really despicable human being." - crime writer Diane Fanning

Millionaire executive Steven Beard woke up screaming.

Experiencing excruciating pain, he reached down and clutched his stomach. He felt the blood on his hands and panicked. His internal organs were oozing outside his belly.

Beard reached over and called for an ambulance. The paramedics worked in vain to stem his bleeding. The seventy-four-year-old writhed in pain but out of the corner of his eye, he saw his wife Celeste enter the room.

"Oh my God," Celeste said. "Steve! What happened?"

The medics pushed the woman back, not wanting her to interfere in his care.

Chaos ensued as his thirty-seven-year-old wife and her two twin daughters entered the room. Police searched around the premise and found a shell on the ground.

Steven Beard had been shot in his stomach.

But by whom?

Was it the wife who strangely was not sleeping in the same bed. The daughters?

Or would it be Tracey Tarlton, a lesbian lover of Celeste?

"They knew Tracey had pulled the trigger," crime writer Diane Fanning said. "But they suspected someone else was involved. But Tracey just wouldn't talk."

Tarlton harbored a secret from the police. She had fallen in love with Beard's wife, Celeste.

But as Tracey would later find out, there was a lot about Celeste that she didn't know about...

CHAPTER ONE

"Celeste Beard had a very rough childhood," Fanning said. "There was a lot of instability, alcoholic abuse in the family and she really had it rough."

The identity of Beard's biological parents has remained a mystery. She was one of four children raised by adoptive parents, Edwin and Nancy Johnson. Celeste would claim that both Edwin and one of her older adoptive brothers would sexually abuse her from age 4 to 12. Nancy, her adoptive mother, was psychologically unstable and be institutionalized on a regular basis.

On one occasion, Celeste's daughter Kristina would record a conversation she had with Celeste in which she talked about her sexual abuse.

"Do you know what it feels like when you're four years old, you aren't even in kindergarten? Do you know what that does to you?"

Celeste has maintained that both adoptive parents physically abused her when she was a child and that she had tried to kill herself during her early teens. At the age of seventeen, she married Craig Bratcher and gave birth to twins, Jennifer, and Kristina. The relationship with Bratcher was a volatile one, filled with physical assaults and restraining orders. The couple would divorce and Beard would lose custody of the twin daughters.

But Celeste could get men to marry her with ease. Easy come, easy go.

She would go on to marry Henry Wolfe, an Air Force mechanic. Once again, the relationship was tempestuous and Celeste would divorce. She would claim later that her own divorce lawyer gave her money to have a boob job done.

She would then move to Arizona and marry a man named Jimmy Martinez. Celeste had a gutter mouth and would spew vulgarities without any kind of filter. She would refer to Martinez' penis as the "BMW" (Big Mexican wiener) but the two would get divorced despite the alleged size of her husband's package.

By the time Celeste reached her mid-thirties, she was desperate for a better life. She worked as a waitress at the Austin Country Club.

"To use an old-fashioned term," Fanning said. "Celeste Beard was a fortune hunter and she was determined to make her way in the world on the back of someone else."

She would meet the wealthy Steven Beard at the Country Club, fawning over the elderly man as he dined with his wife, Elise.

"At the time, Steven was married to Elise," Fanning said. "And from what everyone was saying, they had a wonderful and happy marriage. Then Elise died of cancer and when that happened Celeste knew what she wanted."

She wanted a rich man.

Steven Beard would do.

CHAPTER TWO

Steven Beard was a self-made millionaire. He served in the Navy and went to college at both TCU and SMU. He started his career in radio advertising in Dallas, literally starting at the bottom. By the 1970s, he had graduated to television and in 1981 he had become the general manager of KBVO in Austin, Texas. Four years later, the station would become one of the first affiliates of the now behemoth Fox Network. The station grew by leaps and bounds and Beard would sell his share in the company which completed his fortune.

Celeste targeted the newly widowed Steven for his money. She preyed upon the loneliness and loss of the TV executive and he fell for her charm.

"She paid attention to him," Steven's daughter Becky Beard said. "That's what she needed at the time. That's what he needed the most was for someone to pay attention to him. And he just went hook, line, and sinker."

Three weeks after his wife died, Steven would take Celeste out on a date.

He took Celeste to Mama Mia's Italian restaurant then they had a nightcap at his mansion. The executive then allowed Celeste to borrow his $50,000 Lexus and drive herself home.

Steven spared no expense in his courtship probably figuring that the he could make up for the age difference between the two of them with money. He courted the thirty-eight years younger woman with an open checkbook which included a $16,000 diamond cocktail ring, a $3,000 wristwatch, and a new SUV.

But Steven's family, specifically his daughter, grew suspicious of Celeste's interest in her father.

"I think it was money," Becky said. "I think Celeste was after his money."

"Celeste was in dire straits," Orange said. "She had nothing but bad luck in life and men but always failed to see her own hand in her circumstance. With Steven, she had an older man who would overlook all of those things. He would be able to use his money to bail Celeste out of her debt, depression and dumb choices."

Steven had enough money to give Celeste a clean slate. Celeste had committed insurance fraud during her time in Arizona with Jimmy Martinez and had a $20,000 restitution bill that Steven ultimately paid for.

He then funded a renewed custody battle for Celeste's twin daughters. She would win the case and become reunited with Jennifer and Kristina. The couple did not inform the teen daughters of their union until later. Celeste would pretend to be Steven's housekeeper until one of her daughters caught the two in a hotel room during the 1993 Super Bowl.

The union did not have the blessing of Steven's family. They all thought she was marrying him for his money. Steven ignored their counsel and decided to marry Celeste. He was smart enough to have a prenuptial agreement drawn out. In the agreement, Celeste would receive over half-million dollars if they divorced but she would receive up to six million upon his death.

CHAPTER THREE

Celeste took immediate advantage of her newly acquired status as Mrs. Steven Beard. She went on a shopping spree after shopping spree, wildly spending money on whatever whims she could dream up.

"She was insane about spending money," Fanning said. "She could have gone a year and a half wearing a different pair of shoes and purse every day and not run out. At one point he gave her one million outright and she went through it in record time, like six months."

A part of the marriage agreement that Celeste didn't like was the fact that she had to play the role of a loving wife. She had no problem putting on appearances anywhere outside the bedroom. But in the bedroom was where the problem lay.

Celeste didn't want to have sex with Steven.

"She married him only for money," Fanning said. "So obviously she didn't find a seventy-five-year-old man attractive. So she really didn't want to be sexually involved with him."

On February 18th, 1995, Steven and Celeste would exchange vows at the Austin Country Club. Their honeymoon night involved a "sex needle" wherein Celeste had to insert a syringe into the base of Steven's penis in order for it to stiffen. She described the practice as "unromantic" and "kind of traumatizing."

In the months that followed, Steven wanted more sex than Celeste could put up with as she would refuse to inject the syringe into his penis. Feeling gypped, Steven would file for divorce four months after the wedding but changed his mind after Celeste came up with the "oral sex solution".

Sunday mornings would be reserved for pleasing Steven sexually, a day she referred to as the "Sunday Suck."

Celeste would do her wifely duties with great reluctance. She told her daughters that there should be no distractions at all during her Sunday morning time with Steven. She wanted to get things over with as fast as she could.

Things were going well for Steven. He was happy to have a hot, younger wife performing sex for him once a week.

That is, he was happy with the happy endings until he started to feel the financial burn.

Steven had given Celeste a $10,000 a month allowance but she thought of that as mere chicken feed. She had three walk-in closets that she lined with hundreds of pair of shoes, each with a purse to match. She would go on $50,000 shopping sprees and lavish her friends with gifts and parties. The couple would also take lavish vacations, on one occasion they visited China for a month where they spent over $100,000.

Steven started his marriage with over twelve million dollars in net worth. After only a year of marriage to Celeste, he was down to a rapidly dwindling eleven million.

Celeste would want more.

Much more.

CHAPTER FOUR

Celeste pressed Steven for even more money. She argued daily that the half-million prenuptial agreement was too low. She pressed Steven for more money and he would not budge. But Celeste would not let the issue go until one day Steven just relented. He wrote Celeste a check for a half-million dollars.

Six months later, Celeste had blown through the money.

Then she wanted more.

At that point, Steven blew up. He threatened to cut off all of her credit cards.

"Celeste told Steven that she was going to kill herself if Steven cut off her money supply," Orange said. "Shopping was like a drug for her. She had to have her daily fix. Just going to a mall to buy a pair of cheap shoes wouldn't do it for her. She had to have it all. Every day."

And now Steven no longer wanted to pay the price.

"She had to buy things in order to feel good," Orange said. "It wouldn't have mattered how much she purchased. It would have never been enough. Nothing would ever have been enough."

The final straw was the Christmas holidays of 1998. Celeste had spent nearly $300,000 dollars over a few weeks. Steven went ballistic and the shit started to hit the fan. Celeste grew more contemptuous of Steven as he questioned her spending. She often referred to him as "the fat bastard" or "the old fool."

"What the hell is that old man still doing alive?" she would cry out.

Celeste would start to act out even more. She would leave the mansion for long stretches and spend time at a weekend home that Steven owned along the river. She would not go there alone as she often entertained her ex-husband, Jimmy Martinez.

Steven would eventually find about her extra-marital trysts and threaten divorce.

This prompted Celeste to threaten suicide as a form of retaliation. She would be sent to a psychiatric facility called St. David.

There she would meet a woman named Tracey Tarlton.

Tracey was a manager at a trendy bookstore called the BookPeople. She was also an unstable mental patient who was looking for a girlfriend. One look at the glamorous Celeste was all it took for Tracey. She had to try her hand at seducing the heterosexual and married woman.

"Tracey was an emotionally unstable woman who had been in and out of hospitals for depression and other disorders for quite some time," Fanning said.

The two hit it off.

Tracey would claim that Celeste was "extremely flirtatious" with her in the beginning. She said that the two first had sex on March 20th, 1999 and that their relationship would continue until the day she would shoot Steven.

The two were not discreet about their romance. A photo of a company get together showed Celeste sitting on her lesbian lover's lap. People at the party would later report seeing the women kissing passionately.

Celeste was not a lesbian but she was willing to engage in a relationship with Tracey in order to get what she wanted. She admitted during an interview with a psychiatrist that she had to drink copious amounts of alcohol in order to prepare herself for sex with Tracey. Her daughters began seeing books about lesbian love around the house.

But while Celeste had to numb herself with alcohol, Tracey needed no such aids.

She was immediately smitten by Celeste and wrote her love letters just weeks after they met.

"Celeste, you are so beautiful," Tracey wrote. "I think about your long, silky body and your incredible, long legs and I just can't stand it. And then I think of your incredible face and I want to...stand outside your building and wait until I get arrested. We won't even talk about what happens when I think about your sweet, tough, sexy voice."

"Celeste had no problem trading sex for favors," Orange said. "So she used her sexuality in order to get Tracey to do her bidding."

And that bidding would be murder.

CHAPTER FIVE

When Celeste returned home, she could no longer hide her contempt for her husband. She would drug his drinks and then sneak out of the home to party with Tracey.

She couldn't just divorce the millionaire, however, as she had signed a pre-nuptial agreement.

"Because Celeste had signed a pre-nuptial agreement," Fanning said. "She was only guaranteed a minimum amount of money if she divorced Steven and he'd already given her that money and she'd blown it."

Celeste's daughters would catch their mother in bed with Tracey on occasion. Steven, always a step behind, would find out about Tracey just like he found out about Martinez. He would catch them sharing a lesbian kiss on the lips and would promptly chase Tracey out of the house.

Tracey feared for the future of their relationship after it became out in the open. She was in love with Celeste and fantasized about sharing a life together.

Celeste knew this and decided to use Tracey as a pawn.

Going into her best drama queen act, she tearfully told Tracey about how Steven would verbally abuse her on a daily basis. His constant belittling would leave her feeling suicidal.

"What are we going to do?" Tracey asked.

"I don't know," Celeste said. "Maybe we could kill him?"

"We?"

The idle talk soon turned serious as Tracey would do anything to keep Celeste in her life. Both women sat down and began discussing various ways of murdering Steven.

Their first idea was using a homemade botulism technique. They set some food aside, allowing it to spoil and rot. The two women then ground up the presumably poisonous substance and sprinkled it on a chili dog that the served to Steven.

Both of them watched in eager anticipation as Steven placed tainted food into his mouth.

"Jesus," Steven said as he munched on the hot dog. "This is delicious!"

After that attempt didn't so much as produce a tummy ache, the two women spiked Steven's Vodka with 190-proof alcohol (everclear).

The old man passed out and then they fastened a plastic bag around his head. The bag did not have the effect they wanted as he breathed just fine as he slept off the alcohol.

Feeling desperate, they decide to sprinkle grounded up sleeping pills and ecstasy tablets over his steak.

"Wow," Steven said as he chewed on the tender steak. "This is delicious!"

Nothing worked and the two inept killers became more desperate.

Celeste went into her drama queen act again. She told Tracey that she was dreading an upcoming trip to Europe.

"He's going to make me sleep with him," Celeste said in tearful disgust. "I just can't take it. I can't take it anymore."

"I want to help," Tracey said.

"Then do something!"

"Like what?"

"Kill him," Celeste said. "Kill him for me"

CHAPTER SIX

Tracey was willing to do anything for her lover. Celeste came over to her place and Tracey showed off her 20-gauge shotgun. Her father had given it to her as a gift and had her name engraved on the bottom.

"We can use this," Tracey said as Celeste looked the gun over in fake admiration.

"Tracey was there to do the bidding of Celeste," Orange said. "Celeste had all of the power in the relationship."

"Celeste planned the killing out very carefully," Fanning said. "She drugged her husband's drink to make sure he fell asleep. She went into the other wing of the house where she could justifiably say she heard nothing. Then she left the doors open so that Tracey could sneak in."

Tracey was more than a willing accomplice. She believed that once Steve was eliminated, she and Celeste could finally be together.

On October 2nd, 1999 Tracey stepped into the bedroom of the Beard home and shot Steven in his stomach.

"I had stepped into a space that was just numb when I went into that bedroom," Tracey recalled. "And I shot him."

Steven looked over and saw that his guts were literally, outside his stomach.

"911, what's your emergency?"

"I need an ambulance," Steven said in a pained voice. "Hurry."

"What's the emergency?"

"My guts just jumped out of my stomach. They blew out. Yeah, they blew out of my stomach. They're lying on my stomach."

"OK, they're lying on your stomach?"

"Yes, I'm in bed. I'm in awful pain. I'm having a hard time figuring out what happened. I don't know what happened. I've never had this happen before."

Steven was shell-shocked. He had slept through the gunshot but awakened to find himself with a hole in his stomach.

Deputy Alan Howard was the first to arrive at the Beard estate. He rang the doorbell and banged on the front door but received no answer.

Heard headed around toward the side window and saw Steven writhing in pain on the bed. He busted through the sliding glass and entered.

Sgt. Gregory Truitt arrived as well and the two officers thought that Steven had a surgical incision of some sort ripped open.

Two women then entered the bedroom, Celeste, and her daughter Kristina. A few minutes later, a deputy found a shotgun shell near the bed.

The medical emergency now had become a designated crime scene.

Police searched the home and found the bathroom ransacked. But they realized that the drawers that were ransacked "looked too deliberate."

"This wasn't a burglary gone bad," one of the deputies said. "It was a murder attempt staged to look like a break-in."

CHAPTER SEVEN

Tracey had performed the shooting in the belief that Celeste would do her part. Part of her job was to remove any and all evidence that

Tracey was even there, one of which involved removing any shell casings.

But Celeste never picked up the shotgun shell.

She did keep quiet when the investigation ensued. Every family member and friend pointed to Tracey as a possible suspect except Celeste.

Police arrived at Tracey's home and asked if she had a gun. The woman agreed and the police requested that they test the rifle.

A ballistics match was made and Tracey would be arrested.

Steven would not die immediately from the gunshot wound.

His condition stabilized after seven surgeries. He would die four days after being released from the hospital as the wound become infected.

Celeste would remain by his side throughout his prolonged hospital stay.

But she also found time to shop, spending an astonishing $660,000 from October 1999 to March of 2000.

Steven would succumb from the wounds in January of 2000. Tracey Tarlton would be tried and convicted to life in prison for his murder.

True to her word, Tracey would remain silent in regards to Celeste's involvement.

But the police kept after her. They would try to reason with Tracey at first. When that didn't work, they would resort to taunting tactics.

"She really doesn't care about you," the police interrogator would say. "You're going to do the time for her crime?"

The police wouldn't let go because they knew Celeste was involved. But they needed Tracey's testimony.

"The first mistake Celeste made was that she wasn't in the same bed as Steven," Orange said. "When medics arrived, she came into the room and was clearly not sleeping with her husband. Surely that would raise a few eyebrows with police."

"They kept pressuring Tracey," Fanning said. "Trying to get her to give up Celeste because they knew there was no reason for Tracey to do this completely on her own."

Tracey would remain silent. She would wait in her jail cell for the visit from the love of her life, Celeste Beard.

But Celeste was not going anywhere near Tracey's cell.

She now had Steven's money. She didn't need anything else.

CHAPTER EIGHT

Celeste would eventually contact Tracey again. She would go into her drama queen act again, only this time the play acting would force Tracey's hand to break up with her.

Celeste then believed she had gotten away with everything scott free. Her lesbian lover had taken the fall for the murder. She now had carte blanche to Steven's estate, selling off one of the properties for a cool two million.

But like a curse that followed her around throughout her life, all of Celeste's ill-gotten gains would be short lived.

Celeste would marry Cole Johnson, a local bartender, and part-time musician she would meet in a bar in Aspen, Colorado.

Problem was that Tracey would find out about the union.

"Tracey became enraged when she read the marriage announcement," Orange said. "Here she was taking the fall for someone that she believed had loved her. Now this woman was off to a honeymoon in Aspen, Colorado. At that point, she had to realize that Steven was the victim and not her. She must have felt a sinking in her stomach at the realization that she was being played for so long."

Tracey informed the warden that she was ready to talk. She would tell the police the full story of what happened that night in Austin.

CHAPTER NINE

Nearly a year after orchestrating her husband's murder, Celeste Beard would be brought to trial and found guilty of first-degree murder.

"It was wonderful," Steven's daughter, Becky Beard said after Celeste's guilty verdict was announced. "It was absolutely wonderful. It was 'thank you, Lord.'"

"What brought Celeste down was greed," Fanning said. "Self-centeredness. And a willingness to do anything she wanted no matter who stood in the way."

"celeste had initially arrived at Steven's estate with one box of all of her possessions," Orange said. "Steven, in turn, gave her a lake house, a mansion, diamond jewelry, and allowed her to no longer have to work for a living. And how did she repay him? She killed his ass."

Steven Beard's family was allowed to address Celeste during sentencing. His son, Steven, told Celeste to go burn in hell.

But Celeste's own daughter turned on her.

"You say we turned on you," Kristina said. "Well, you turned on us. You turned on the whole Beard family. He let you into his home, loved you, honored, obeyed you, and you violated him and murdered him...Shame on you!"

Celeste will not be eligible for parole until the age of 80. She did not receive the six million "owed" to her after Steven's death. The proceeds of the Beard estate went toward his own children but also to Celeste's daughters, whom he had adopted.

Celeste continues to deny her involvement and now blames her incarceration on her daughters.

"They had two million reasons to lie," she said from her jail cell.

SHE MATES, SHE KILLS: THE TRUE STORY OF TAUSHA MORTON

49

ALISON YALE

AN AGGRESSIVE FLIRT

Dewayne Barrentine met Tausha Morton in early 2007.

She worked as a teacher's assistant at his son's daycare. A single parent, Barrentine would pick up his son and would be greeted by Tausha on a daily basis.

"Whenever I would pick him up," Barrentine said. "She would always make sure to step out into the hallway and give him a hug and say 'hey' to me. She made herself very noticeable."

Tausha gave Barrentine all of the hints that she was interested. The sideways glance, the smile that lingered just a little too long. But still, he needed extra coaxing.

"One of her co-workers actually approached me," Barrentine recalled when a woman in the hallway had passed him a note.

"She said, 'It's a phone number,' I said, 'To who?' She said 'Miss Tausha and she wants you go give her a call tonight. And it started from there."

Smitten by the forward nature of the sweet-faced single mother, Barrentine fell hard.

The two began dating and began living together within a month.

"She was really there for my son...," Barrentine recalled. "I had full custody of him. He would lay in the bed next to me ... and I would hear him say his prayers and he would pray for a mama." He would soon feel the same way about Tausha's daughter, Lexie.

"We weren't dating even a month and she said, 'Will you be my daddy?' And I said, 'Baby, I'll be whatever you want me to be...'"

From that moment, Barrentine became hooked as Tausha made him feel as if she really loved him. She did all the little things from kind words to love letters.

He soon began to realize, however, that Tausha had a manipulative, lying nature.

The tall tales began to pile up. She told Barrentine that she had a "Bachelor's degree in Criminal Justice" as well as an inheritance due to her from an inhertiance.

"It was from her granddad who was a federal judge who was blinded by a battery blowing up in his face. If he was a federal judge, surely his name would be on docs under Google somewhere, but I never found anything."

Barrentine grew increasingly suspicious with Tausha's stories. He did some online investigating and discovered that she had a previous marriage with a man named Mitch Kemp. He confronted her about it and she would state that she had been married five times before.

The two vaguely resembled each other, big Southern boys, "teddy bears" that were more than a little overweight.

After eight months of co-habitation, Barrentine caught Tausha cheating on him.

He promptly threw her out of his home.

"I called the Sheriff's department," Barrentine recalled. "I was like, 'look, I don't care what y'all do with her, she's got to get her shit and get outta my house.'"

Wanting retribution of some sort, Barrentine accessed Tausha's MySpace account as he knew her password.

"Dewayne gets on her Myspace account basically to mess with her," prosecutor Richard Hicks said.

After sifting through her e-mails, Barrentine would make a shocking discovery.

"I found two or three e-mails," Barrentine said. "And they were from Mitch Kemp's sister-in-law."

Mischele Kemp had written Tausha an e-mail with the subject "We're really concerned."

"How is Mitch doing? We haven't heard from you in over our year? We would like to hear from you. If we don't hear from you immediately we will contact law enforcement and media. It is not like Mitch to disappear for years on end without contacting his mother and we have became extremely concerned. Please contact us. We are very worried about him and your entire family. Sincerely, MK."

Digging a little deeper, Barrentine looked into Tausha's "sent message" box and it did not appear that she had ever responded.

"Immediately, I changed the password on the account," Barrentine said. "To where she couldn't access it and I printed off all those e-mails."

His actions would prove to be something bigger than a missing persons case. He would bring all of this information to the local police chief in Florida who instructed him to keep things to himself as he sorted things out with the Boone County Sheriff's Department in Missouri.

WHO WAS TAUSHA MORTON?

Tausha Morton, AKA Tausha Fields, met Mitch Kemp in 2001 when she lived in Colombia, Missouri.

Mitch worked as a carpet installer and had been recently divorced after fourteen years of marriage.

"It wasn't long after he got divorced that he met Tausha," Mitch's brother Rick said. "I would say within months."

Despite their eleven year age difference, Kemp fell hard for the young and vivacious Tausha.

Tausha was the proverbial "people person." Most of her friends and neighbors described her as someone who would make you welcome and treat you as if you were a long lost friend.

"She was bubbly," said one of Tausha's former employers. "Friendly and inquisitive. She paid attention and asked lots of questions about you."

Tausha liked learning about other people. She, in turn, would be all too willing to share details of her own struggles.

"She told us how her whole family was killed in a car accident," Rick Kemp said.

Tausha had a way of getting people to feel sorry for her. She would come across as a heavily burdened individual who suffered a lot of tragedy. People listening to her story would feel compassion for her lot in life and do what they could to help her.

Mitch Kemp listened intently to Tausha's tales of woe, buying them hook, line and sinker. He wanted to help her. To be her rescuer, her knight in shining armor.

The two began to date and by September of 2002, Tausha gave birth to a baby girl.

Mitch loved kids and was ecstatic. He proposed marriage and Tausha accepted.

"They got married in Pensacola," Rick said. "It was a very easy wedding."

The marriage seemed to look okay from all observers. Mitch's family didn't have any misgivings about Tausha, her charm enabling her to get into their good graces, at least at first.

"She was a really sweet girl," Carole Kemp said, recalling her first meeting with Tausha.

But over time, his family began to notice a personality change in Mitch. Sister Mischelle stated that he wasn't "as playful as he used to be."

Family gatherings would "take a back seat to things that she wanted to do" according to Tracy Kemp, who blamed Tausha's ability to manipulate.

As work responsibilities increased for Mitch, things began to go south in their marriage very fast.

DOMESTIC LIFE AIN'T FOR ME

Bored that she was left alone with the baby, the high-strung Tausha needed an outlet.

She would arrive at her friend's gym, the Body Zone, with her baby in tow. Soon she began working part time at the fitness center.

It was there that she would meet Greg Morton.

Morton was more physically fit than Kemp but he fit the same profile psychologically. He had recently broken up with a longtime girlfriend and was be vulnerable to the manipulative charms of Tausha.

"Greg was despondent over his break-up," a family friend said. "But when he met Tausha, he kinda perked back up."

Tausha used the same seductive strategy on Morton as she used on Kemp. She detailed her tragic back story. She told him stories of being molested, of being raped.

She also told Morton in no uncertain terms that her marriage with Kemp was on the outs. Making herself look like the victim, she told Morton that Kemp had made her miserable. He was abusive, bothered her constantly and threatened physical harm.

"She told him a bunch of lies," one of Tausha's friends said. "She said she was getting him (Mitch) served, that they were getting divorced."

By February 2004, her allegations of physical abuse would be reported to the police department as Tausha filed assault charges against him.

"She said he abused her," Rick Kemp said. "By assaulting her, or slapping her or something."

Tausha informed police that she and Mitch had gotten into an argument. Then he hauled off and hit her.

Mitch Kemp would plead guilty to the charges and spend over a month in jail. Upon his release, he would be in for another surprise.

Tausha had moved out of the family home and moved in with Greg Morton, taking Lexie with her. Morton had own a farm outside of Colombia, Missouri, a sizable estate that he inherited from his step-father.

A custody battle then ensued between Tausha and Mitch for their daughter. The fight would get uglier by the day with daily phone calls between the two and their attorneys. She would refuse to allow Mitch to see Lexie and used the courts to prevent visitation.

But Mitch Kemp would not give up without a fight.

"If he had to go through the court system to do it, he would do it," Mitch's brother Rick said. "But that he was going to see his daughter."

Tausha would state that their divorce was finalized in August as the custody battle lingered on. She would then marry Greg Morton the same month.

But Morton had no idea what he was getting into and a "triangle" domestic dispute ensued.

Tausha had arranged to meet with Mitch in order to get some personal belongings. She drove in with Greg to the house of Mitch's friend where he was staying. Mitch confronted Tausha on the front porch where he immediately berated her, screaming insults.

Greg was waiting in the car at the time and went to intervene on Tausha's behalf. Mitch became further enraged and hit Greg over the head with a patio chair.

Retreating, Greg and Tausha sprinted back to the car.

Mitch, however, would disappear after that confrontation.

THE DISAPPEARANCE OF MITCH KEMP

It took awhile for Mitch's disappearance to hit home for his family members and friends. He was the type of man whom you would not hear from from awhile but would suddenly show up on the front porch.

He was dutiful about calling his mother Carole and when she didn't hear from him, she began to worry.

"We called the Boone County Sheriff's office," Rick Kemp said. "About two weeks afterward, probably. We told them that Mitch had disappeared."

The Sheriff's department did not think any foul play was involved. They offered assurance to the family that Mitch "probably didn't want to be found."

Boone County detectives came to that conclusion after they found out that Mitch was wanted for stealing some goods from a friend. They believed he disappeared in order to escape from repercussions of his actions.

Meanwhile, Greg and Tausha were living large. In late 2004, Greg put up his farm for sale which surprised both his friends and family. He treasured the land as it was bequeathed to him from his stepfather. Those close to him believed that Tausha had put him up to it.

In February of 2005, the sale of the farm finalized. With a $275,000 payout in hand, he and Tausha left Missouri, telling no one.

The Kemp family continued to believe that Mitch was not missing and that Tausha was involved somehow. They just didn't have any evidence or clues. Just a damn strong suspicion.

"Something had either happened to Mitch that had nothing to do with Tausha," Rick Kemp said. "Or something happened to Mitch and Tausha had something to do with it."

Both the Kemp family and Boone County law enforcement would then find locating Tausha and Greg to be a fruitless exercise. They literally disappeared from the face of the earth, wanting a new life. Leaving no trail behind, Tausha and Greg would move all the way to the Gulf Coast.

Greg, still smitten by Tausha, would get a tattoo of her name on his back as if he were a branded cow. With a new man firmly under her control, Tausha would go on a spending spree which included getting breast implants with Greg's money.

NO SIGN OF MITCH

By February of 2008, the Kemp family still had not heard from Mitch.

"They took a missing persons report," Rick Kemp said. "But the case went cold, quite frankly, because they didn't do anything about it."

But the Kemp family would not give up hope. They continued their search, turning to the Internet to look for any trace of their beloved son and brother.

They would search different social networking sites and court systems to look for any trace of Mitch.

They found nothing for years.

Until Mischelle Kemp found Tausha on MySpace, the social networking account.

"My sister-in-law found an account," Rick Kemp said. "That had Tausha's name and picture on it."

Mischelle immediately sent Tausha an e-mail.

"Tausha didn't respond," Rick Kemp said. "But Dewayne Berrentine did."

REVENGE SEEKING BOYFRIEND TO THE RESCUE

Dewayne Berrentine read through Tausha's e-mails on MySpace and began connecting the dots.

"Her little stories," Berrentine said. "Just because somebody lies to me, that doesn't mean I'm going to call you out on it immediately. I thought that she was coming up with these stories to impress me, maybe?"

Dewayne had discovered that Tausha had gotten around. He received some disturbing information from a man that Tausha had dated after she met Greg and before she met Dewayne.

His name was Keith Jones.

"I was in love with her and anything else didn't matter," Jones recalled. "You couldn't verify anything that she said," he says. "You know, and I mean there were a lot of stories."

Keith and Dewayne exchanged notes and stories about Tausha. They realized that she told them the same outlandish stories. But then Jones told Dewayne a story that he didn't hear before.

He described how Tausha revealed to him that she was involved in the murder of one of her exes.

"She had a few drinks in her," Jones recalled. "She said this guy had raped her and her daughter. And she apparently ... went to where he was and lured him back to her house ... and he walked in the front door. And that's when Greg shot him in the chest."

Both men thought the story was "so far-fetched" and because of the lies they always heard from her, thought nothing of it.

Dewayne did eventually confront Tausha about the allegation and she dismissed it out of hand, saying that her ex-boyfriend would say anything to throw a wrench into her new relationship.

Dewayne would change his mind about things when he opened Mischelle Kemp's e-mail message to Tausha, however. After notifying the authorities, he also wrote Mischelle Kemp back who in turn contacted the authorities in Boone County. The Sheriff's department then reopened the case. After doing some sniffing around, they discovered that Mitch had "fallen off the face of the earth" and had not filed taxes in over four years.

Finally, the Boone County Sheriff department realized that something was wrong.

INVESTIGATING TAUSHA

Detectives decided to start researching the background of Tausha.

They would discover that Tausha's parents were alive contrary to her account that they were both dead. Mitch's mother had spoken to Tausha's father shortly before her soon was to be married.

"She said, 'Mitch, we need to talk,'" recalled Rick Kemp. "You've heard a bunch of stories. Her family wasn't killed in a car wreck. They're alive. They don't want anything to do with Tausha. They say she's nothing but trouble."

Mitch dismissed the notion of his mother. He was totally smitten with Tausha.

Further investigations would reveal that Tausha had been married and divorced twice by the time she met Mitch Kemp. She would go onto have four marriages before she was thirty and the number of men she lived were numerous. Mitch had no idea that Tausha went from one man to the next man to the next. Even if he did, he was so smitten by her early in their relationship that he would have probably ignored the red flags.

Investigators would further discover that her divorce to Kemp was never finalized so she may have married Greg Morton while she was still married to Kemp.

Tracking her movements after she moved from Missouri proved difficult. Tausha and Greg were eventually tracked to Alabama.

The couple lived an indulgent lifestyle, buying luxury homes and cars on the $275,000 sale they profited after selling the farm.

But it didn't take long for them to blow through the money.

Needing more income to support Tausha, Greg would go to Mississippi in the hopes of finding clean-up work after Hurricane Katrina hit. After he left, Tausha saw it as an opportunity to cut him loose.

She had to find someone new.

"While he was gone doing Katrina," Barrentine said. "She was blowing through his money. Then he came home finding another man laying in his bed and he's broke."

Greg would immediately file for divorce.

MEN AND MORE MEN

Cut off from her money supply from Greg, Tausha would find work as an assistant at a day care center. It was there that she would meet Dewayne Barrentine.

She would follow the same modus operandi in her seduction of Barrentine, telling him the sob stories of her life. She described how Greg Morton would abuse her and how she escaped. She gave details on how Greg would try to "jump on her" and that they had "several physical altercations."

Agreeing to let her move in, Dewayne would meet Greg when he was helping Tausha get her belongings out of his house.

The two didn't fight. Instead, they spoke briefly and Greg would later tell Dewayne about how detectives from Missouri were looking to speak with Tausha.

Barrentine would eventually discover Tausha cheating on him and throw her out of his home. She would find a new boyfriend a few days later by the name of Denver Workman.

Workman left his job and his extended family from Florida to Wilmington, Delaware after Tausha begged him to do so. Then she wanted him to move back and Workman refused.

"She would yell, scream and throw things at me because I wasn't leaving," Workman recalled. "She would tell Lexie I was a bad person and to kick me. I bought her a bus ticket to Florida and let her borrow my truck that was still down there. She took the truck, and I never saw her again."

Police would finally catch up to Tausha in Dothan, Alabama and confront her about the disappearance of Mitch Kemp.

During her initial interrogation, Tausha would firmly deny having any contact with Mitch.

"What do you mean what happened to Mitch?" Tausha would ask detectives in bewilderment. "I haven't had any contact with him. None."

The investigators continued to press, however, and Tausha would try to insinuate Greg as having something to do with Mitch's disappearance.

"They had words on the phone," Tausha told detectives. "And then they had, they got in a fist fight one time."

After being threatened with the possibility of being put in jail and leaving her five year old daughter Lexie in the hands of the state, Tausha then placed the blame on Greg.

"Greg killed Mitch," Tausha said. "He told me."

She would then inform detectives that she wasn't there when it happened. She stated that Greg left about 45 minutes later after he had yet another phone conversation with Mitch.

Tausha would claim that she feared for both her and her child's life because of Greg's temper.

She would recall that Greg shot Mitch on the farm. Investigators played along, even paying for her plane ticket to fly from Alabama to Missouri in order to let them know where Greg had buried Mitch. But once she arrived, Tausha seemed confused by the layout of the farm. She could not pinpoint where exactly the body had been buried.

She was then released under her own recognizance back to Alabama while Sheriff deputies proceeded to dig up the farm to no avail. They used ground penetrating radar, cadaver sniffing dogs but came up empty.

WHERE WAS GREG MORTON?

While talks with Tausha revealed some clues, investigators were even more eager to speak with Greg Morton.

After ending his marriage with Tausha, he settled in St. Louis. He was going to school to become an electrician and had a new girlfriend.

He wanted nothing further to do with Tausha. When investigators approached him, Greg immediately invoked his right to an attorney and refused to speak further.

Detectives did not have enough evidence to charge him. But they had Tausha on the run and spoke to her again. This go around, they decided to employ a little psychological manipulation.

"But I tell you what," Detective Dave Wilson said while sitting across from Tausha in the interrogation room. "He (Greg Morton) automatically assumed that you talked to us. Now, we didn't confirm that."

"Why did he think that?" Tausha asked.

"Well, there's only...who knows?"

"But he said he thought he'd talk to you?"

"I'm going to ask you again. Can you take us directly to where that hole was?"

This go around, Tausha said yes. The Boone County Sheriff's department flew her in from Alabama yet again to Greg Morton's farm.

This time, Tausha led investigators straight to where the body was buried.

Mitch Kemp's remains were dug up and his identity was confirmed.

"It didn't surprise us," Rick Kemp said. "But we were all just blown away. I mean, I just didn't want to believe that my brother was gone."

Investigators discovered that Mitch had been shot numerous times and found numerous shell casings in the makeshift grave. They then went to St. Louis and arrested Greg Morton.

"He wasn't surprised when we showed up," Detective Wilson recalled.

Tausha was allowed to return home but investigators had a suspicion that she was more involved than she let on.

A VOW OF SILENCE

Greg strangely refused to rat out Tausha, remaining in prison until he was officially charged.

Tausha moved to Texas, however, and began dating someone new. Investigators would catch up with her again, however, and this time a heated ninety-minute interrogation would ensue.

Their probing questions would force Tausha to change her story about Mitch's murder completely.

"I did not do anything," Tausha said after detectives informed her that she would be charged with first-degree murder. "I helped you in every way I could possibly fucking help you.

"Tausha," Detective Wilson said slowly. "We got people who say, say otherwise, okay."

Tausha then changed her story again, stating that she was present when Greg murdered Mitch.

"I snuck around behind Greg's back and I saw Mitch, okay," Tausha said. "Greg had no idea."

She stated Greg would kill Mitch in a jealous rage after they returned from a hotel for a tryst. They then drove back to the farm and Greg assaulted Mitch before he got out of the car.

"He had a gun in his hands," Tausha said. "It was a black gun. Mitch started walking backwards. I ran inside the house and then I ran back outside. I saw that Mitch was walking backwards, and Greg was walking towards him. And Greg shot him. I didn't kill Mitch. I didn't want Mitch to die."

But the investigators didn't see it that way. They charged her with first-degree murder.

THE TRIAL

In June of 2009, Tausha had been imprisoned for over six months as she awaited trial.

Her bail was set at one million dollars.

Greg Morton then decided it was time to cut a deal. He broke his silence on what really happened the day of Mitch Kemp's murder. He would admit to his involvement in exchange for a more lenient sentence if he testified against Tausha.

In 2010, Tausha's trial began.

The prosecution's argument was that Tausha was the mastermind behind the murder, that even though Greg pulled the trigger it was Tausha that put the idea in his head. They also believed that Tausha's motive was to have sole custody of their daughter.

The defense would claim that Tausha was innocent and the victim. Her attorney was, in essence, using the same technique that Tausha used on all of her men. They would play on sympathy and hope that the jury would be as charmed by Tausha as all of her men.

GREG MORTON CONFESSES

Morton would take the stand and tell the jury exactly how Tausha manipulated him to kill Mitch.

"She's hysterical," Morton recalled. "She said Mitch raped her."

"What are you feeling, Greg, at this point?" Prosecutor Hicks asked.

"I wanted retribution. Tausha took charge and handed me a gun the net morning. She goes, 'I'm going to get Mitch, and when I get back, you shoot him.'"

"What were you going to do, Greg?"

"I was going to do what she asked me to do."

"They made a plan in that Tausha was going to go in town and pick Mitch up," Rick Kemp said. "And tell him that Greg was out of town."

Mitch arrived at the farm, thinking that it would only be the two of them. But then Greg emerged from the porch.

"I had a gun in my hand," Morton recalled. "I raised it and pointed it at him. I kinda paused I was kinda struggling with it a little bit. And then she started yelling at me to shoot him."

Greg believed that he was committing a protective act. He believed that Mitch was raping Tausha and molesting their six-year-old daughter.

"Then she said 'You got to get something to move him. Get something to move him with." Greg recalled. "Then she said, 'Come on. You should have had this ready.'"

"And you saw that she was still struggling?"

"He was."

"So what did you do?"

"I shot him again."

"Was he struggling anymore?"

"It was over," Morton said. "I used farm equipment to pick up Mitch's body and we buried him in a pit. When we were rolling the dirty on Mitch she said 'Mitch Kemp is a piece of shit and nobody is going to look for him for a long time.'"

The defense would then call a neighbor who testified on Tausha's behalf, stating that she thought she was under Greg's control.

Greg then broke down on the stand and tearfully apologized to Mitch Kemp's family.

Over time, however, he began to realize that Tausha was a cunning liar. As he got to know her better, he realized that he had been duped.

"He'd been played like a fiddle by her," Rick Kemp said. "She did it to every man that she had."

Tausha was not called to the stand by the defense and the jury would find her guilty.

"I think she thought she was going to walk," Rick Kemp said. "She thought she could just get away with lying and manipulating people."

Tausha Morton was sentenced to life in prison without parole but is currently appealing her sentencing.

SHEILA LABARRE

PROLOGUE

The farmhouse and surrounding area looked like something from the set of "Little House on the Prairie."

The house on Harvey Farm stood nestled in between tall pine trees, peaceful streams, and wildlife.

A place where you don't expect to find scenes that would be given an "X" rating if it were a horror movie.

The police arrived at the home while conducting a search for a missing young man named Kenneth Countje. They did not have to search far to find evidence of criminal activity. In the front of the property, lay a mattress burning alongside a smoking garbage barrel.

Their first inclination was to believe that the resident was burning garbage. A citation was due, maybe, but they had more pressing matters to attend to.

But upon closer inspection of the barrel, the officers saw a bone sticking out of the garbage.

A femur?

A mass of fleshy goo remained at the knob of the bone and the smell of the charred remains made the policemen gag.

They both gave each other a look of horror. Here in a town where the most serious crime would be a speeding ticket or jaywalking, the police were about to enter a whole world of horror beyond their wildest imagination.

CHAPTER ONE

Epping, New Hampshire.

Population = less than six thousand.

Epping is a rainy, small town that has been sarcastically nicknamed "The Center of the Universe". That has not stopped the residents from hosting parades, canoe races and music festivals. But when Sheila LaBarre arrived, the tiny hamlet soon became known for murder.

"She was a smart woman," forensic psychologist Paula Orange said. "Not book smart but intuitive. She could read people."

Sheila was born Sheila Kaye Bailey in Fort Payne, Alabama in 1958.

She was the youngest of six children. Her first marriage with a man named Ronnie Jennings would last less than two months. Jennings would find out that Sheila had been locking his child from a previous marriage in a closet to punish her. Jennings would divorce Sheila but she would find herself a new man in short order, tying the knot with John Baxter and moving to Chattanooga, Tennessee. Even though married, she would secretly fantasize about being swept away by a rich man. Sheila's mental illness would come to bear in her second marriage and that would end in divorce as well. Despondent, Sheila tried to kill herself and was sent to a psychiatric facility. She would be raped by an orderly inside the hospital.

Now single in Tennessee, the cash-strapped Sheila was forced to live in a local YMCA. She attended a church service and had a private talk with one of the preachers as she wanted "spiritual guidance." She would later claim that the reverend asked if she wanted to "sit in his lap." She then went to a psychiatrist who asked her if she had anal sex with any of her former husbands. The doctor then called Sheila at home and asked if "what she was wearing" and if she "was touching herself."

"If what we are to believe all of Sheila's stories," Orange said. "Then literally all of her interactions with men have ended with them as the pervert and her as the victim. Her sister would later testify that Sheila was molested by her father when she was young. Then her abusive marriages, the rape at the psych facility segues into a spiritual search where she meets a preacher who shows her the tent in his pants. Crazy."

CHAPTER TWO

Sheila turned to personal ads after her failures in marriage. She didn't like the normal courtship process of going to bars and meeting men there. She used the personal ads to cherry pick the men she wanted, men she could dominate.

"Whether on-line or off-line, Sheila behaved like a woman who was in complete control," Orange said. "She would develop a strange kind of power over men. It was almost as if she knew which men would be vulnerable to her feminine wiles and which ones would fight back. But when it came to Dr. Bill LaBarre, it was more of a case of getting the money."

While in Tennessee, Dr. LaBarre decided to take out a personal ad. He would get a response from Sheila who immediately sought to separate herself from the other paramours of the rich doctor.

She sent the doctor nude Polaroids of herself.

The strategy worked.

"She showed no shame in flirting with the older man and soon had him in the palm of her hand," Orange said. "He'd buy her fancy clothes, necklaces, the whole nine yards."

Wilfred "Bill" LaBarre was a successful chiropractor but lonely. Overweight and bespectacled, he had little to offer aside from his wealth. He was in his sixties and recently widowed.

Dr. Labarre was considered a good man by all who knew him. He had been the "Chiropractor of the Year" in 1983 but that would be the same year his beloved Edwina would pass away from cancer. Eager to salve the loneliness, he married another woman named Leona but she abandoned the doctor after a few years. He had two children from his first marriage; Laura and Gregory.

Now alone and widowed, the doctor wanted to spend his golden years enjoying his wealth.

And a young woman.

He would look at the nude Polaroids of the curvaceous Southern Belle, becoming obsessed.

"Here was a lonely, older man who all of a sudden had a 27-year old woman sending him nude photos. He thought he hit the jackpot."

Dr. LaBarre soon invited Sheila to come live with him at his farm in Epping, New Hampshire. The farm was a spacious one, a 115-acre horse ranch that according to LaBarre, "needed a female hand."

Sheila would become enamored by life on the farm, at least at first. She "never heard a June bug before" and the isolated country home gave her a peace that she never experienced.

Neighbors were not shocked that Dr. LaBarre took in such a younger woman as his girlfriend. He reportedly had other girlfriends after his wife died. "Sheila ran all the other girls off," one neighbor said.

But Sheila would prove to be a high-maintenance girlfriend. She would drain Dr. LaBarre's finances, making him buy her gifts and prizes which included a brand-new Silver Mercedes.

She also began to interject herself into LaBarre's estate and business dealings.

The farm that LaBarre owned was called the Old Harvey Farm. It was named after the original owners of the property who still lived in the area. But Sheila forced the doctor to change the name, she wanted it called something that reflected her personality.

The Silver Leopard Farm.

Sheila then had a sign made up and had it placed at the entrance.

She was marking her territory.

CHAPTER THREE

Despite the constant gifts and financial prizes, Sylvia proved to be an ungrateful sugar baby. The relationship would turn tempestuous after a few months. Sheila would claim that Dr. LaBarre often referred to himself as an "old fart" and looked the other way when Sheila began to have different men over for sex.

"He just worried about me when I would date far from home. But he was getting old and his heart would stop beating sometimes."

But the couple fought and police were routinely called to the residence to mediate their domestic disputes.

"You would sometimes hear gunshots," Bruce Allen, a LaBarre neighbor said. "You would hear her screaming, 'I'm going to kill you, you mother fucker!'"

Sheila once pulled a gun on the doctor and forced him out of the home. The chiropractor hid behind a boulder as his girlfriend shot at him.

LaBarre's daughter also recalled that she heard Sheila screaming threats at her father. "I'm gonna kill the horses and I'm going to kill you too."

Laura would later remark at how much her father changed after Sheila came into his life. He went from a normal, well-liked member of the community to a meek, submissive man.

"Sheila was all about being an opportunist," Orange said. "She had the ability to read a man, analyzing his weaknesses, size him up and then push the buttons. With LaBarre, she had a lonely man in front of her. He would tolerate anything in order not to lose her at first and then he simply became fearful of his life. These men in this small New England town did not have the wherewithal to deal with a violent sociopath like Sheila."

Sheila didn't stop with the renaming of Old Harvey Home. She soon took over the accounting duties at LaBarre's chiropractic business. She began organizing the practice into a well-oiled machine. She would track down patients who owed the doctor money and file numerous small claims in the Hampton District Court.

Concerned friends would advise him to dump Sheila before it was too late but it became apparent that the doctor either didn't know how or was afraid to. Dr. LaBarre informed neighbor Bruce Allen that he "had to get rid of her" and that he wanted to "send her back to Alabama. Hopefully, she'll stay there."

Her power over Dr. LaBarre increased to the point where he had given her power of attorney. She began rewriting his will, becoming the executor of his estate. The will stated that he was leaving everything to "a very special lady known as Sheila Kaye Jennings LaBarre."

"The will was very carefully redacted from the original," Orange said. "She kept a lot of the parts of the original and used her own typewriter to amend the little detail of where all the assets will go to. She was very astute and covered her tracks very well for someone who was supposedly schizophrenic."

The two would live together (Sheila would move out briefly but claim to be his common-law wife) from 1987 until LaBarre's death in 2000 at the age of 74. The coroner logged his cause of death as heart disease. There were suspicions among those close to the doctor that believe Sheila poisoned him to hasten the process.

"He was pretty old," Orange said. "And according to the autopsy, the heart disease was significant. So Sheila didn't have anything to do with his death despite the suspicions. The killings would come later."

Sheila would inherit the farm, LaBarre's Chiropractor office, two apartments and a rental home.

This was all valued at over two million dollars in assets.

Strangely, Sheila would marry a Jamaican national named Wayne Ennis in August of 1995 while living with Dr. LaBarre. Ennis drove a tour bus around Jamaica and Sheila made sure that when she toured the islands with Dr. LaBarre that they would cross paths with her Jamaican lover. She arranged for Ennis to obtain a visa and took him back to the farm with her. She would later claim that she and the doctor had stopped having sex and that she "had needs" which apparently Ennis took care of. She would later concede to pleasing the doctor sexually, "I'd use my hand," she said afterward.

Ennis would live in the farmhouse for almost a year. He had his own numerous encounters with Sheila which were violent and bizarre. One night, she ordered him to get in the car. The two then drove around the quiet town, Sheila's voice taking on a conspiratorial tone.

"I wish one of those damn horses would just kick him (Dr. LaBarre) in the head," Sheila said. "Kick him in the head and kill his old ass. I've thought about strangling him myself. But now I have a better idea. I want you to kill him."

Ennis was too frightened to say no to Sheila. The two would eventually divorce and the court records reveal that Sheila took out a restraining order against him.

Ennis disputed the allegations and stated that Sheila was the abuser.

He would later recall being punched, pushed, and shot at by Sheila.

"She told me that she was going to send me back to Jamaica in a box," Ennis said.

Dr. LaBarre told Ennis that Sheila was crazy and believed that she would eventually kill him. He gave the Jamaican money and sent him to the bus station, requesting that he leave town for his own safety.

After the relationship with Ennis ended, Sheila began dating James Brackett.

She and James would remain together for six years despite the fact that Sheila would attack Brackett with a pair of scissors, a machete, and an ax. When all of that failed she tried to shoot him.

The two would break up after which Brackett would get himself a vanity license plate that read "I'm Alive."

Brackett recalled moments where Sheila would act sweet and nice only to go into a violent rage moments later. He said that the greatest example was a time when he was taking a long bath with Sheila only to have her get out of the tub and smash him in the face with a two-foot grill brush.

Two of his teeth would be knocked out from the impact.

Sheila would attack Brackett for a variety of transgressions that would not be guilty of. Hurting her rabbits, damaging her property or having affairs with other women.

Brackett finally had enough, escaping from the farm on one rainy night and hitchhiking back into town.

"I'm lucky to be alive," he would later state.

CHAPTER FOUR

Sheila inherited the farm after LaBarre's death. The doctor's children tried to contest the will but were told that the odds of winning the case were 50/50 at best. They would also have to front over $50,000 to pay for the court costs.

Sheila soon turned the farm into her own private fiefdom. She would hire young men to help her around the place then pay them with her sexual favors or sometimes just beat the shit out of them.

"There would neighbors that would claim to see young men leave her house," Orange said. "They would look beaten up; black eyes, bloody lips, facial contusions. God knows what else."

Her neighbors began to suspect something fishy was going on but had no real evidence to call the police with.

"The first time I met Sheila LaBarre was at the Harvey Farm Stand," said Bonnie Meroth, one of Sheila's neighbors. "It was during the summertime when the produce was ready. I had no basic interaction with her except that of someone standing next to another person as a consumer. And she suddenly turned around and said 'I'll kill you if you come down to my farm' or words to that effect."

Bonnie would later claim that Sheila would try to scare her while driving down the road, nearly running her over while she was on her morning walk.

When she wasn't intimidating neighbors and townsfolk, Sheila would use the farm as the playground for her own private fetishes.

She liked to control and bully men. Stroking one of her pet rabbits, she would punish and insult the men unlucky enough to work at her farm.

"Are you kidding me?" Sheila yelled at the young man who dropped the wheelbarrow. "This should have been done yesterday."

He was young and naive, needing money. If it meant taking lip from Sheila, so be it. He needed work and she seemed nice when she hired him.

"Hurry up!" Sheila said, kicking the man in his buttocks. "Move, move. Are you kidding me? I've never seen a lazier man in my life."

Fatigued after working sixteen hours for seven days straight, the young man keeled over in exhaustion, dropping the wheelbarrow.

"Bitch made, perverted ass pedophile!" Sheila said. "Is this what I am paying you for? I am paying you to work. Now get off your bitch ass. Now!"

It became apparent that Sheila had a gift. A gift of controlling a certain type of man. Verbally abusive and overbearing, she encountered very little resistance.

She kicked the young man again. "Your name is 'bitch', you hear me?"

His real name was Michael Deloge.

CHAPTER FIVE

Deloge had problems as a teen. He got caught up in drugs and found himself on the streets, living out of homeless shelters. In 2004, he would meet Sheila LaBarre.

Deloge became smitten with the woman whom he saw as the life of the party. She would drink beer and play country songs on a guitar. According to Deloge's stepfather, Gordon Boston, the duo would indulge in drugs and study "sadistic material".

Deloge would join Sheila at her farm and soon become her personal whipping boy. Sheila would slap him around like a rag doll. One of the fellow ranch hands, Philip Sullos, recalled witnessing Sheila beating on Deloge with a hardwood stick until he bled. Deloge cowered and took the beating. She would then throw Deloge into a windowless shack and slam the door shut.

Deloge would cower meekly in the corner until Sheila came and got him, making no attempt to escape.

He would be declared missing in 2004 and no one would ever see him again.

In February of 2006, Sheila began looking for a new farmhand. She had her own criteria. He had to be young but pliable to her controlling methods.

She would find the perfect foil in Kenny Countie.

"Kenny was a lovely boy," Carolynn Lodge, Kenny's mother said. "He couldn't do enough for you. Everyone was his friend. I was so proud of him. He never had a horrible word for anybody and that was the problem. He trusted everybody."

Kenny's trust would lead him into Sheila LaBarre's trap.

Kenny would answer one of Sheila's personal ads. The young man was still naive and according to some reports had a "low IQ". The two met through a telephone personal ad service with Sheila calling up the young man and charming him in a way that no woman ever did.

"He (Kenny) told my son Brian that he met a 47-year old woman in New Hampshire," Lodge said. "She owned a farm. She owned a beautiful car. And she was rich. And he was serious about her."

"Kenny fit Sheila's psychological criteria," Orange said. "She targeted men whom she could overpower not only physically but also mentally. She was older than Kenny and light years more cunning. She knows exactly what to say and do to push his buttons. She takes the lead, telling him that he is going to be 'in for the time of his life' and that she 'can't wait to see him.' To a young man with limited experience and intelligence like Kenny, this is music to his ears."

Sheila would arrive at Kenny's home in the silver Mercedes. The silver leopard, the cougar, picking up her prey and taking him back to her lair.

Kenny's family would never see him again.

Sheila would use the same methods on Kenny as she did on the men in the past. She seduced the young man first then isolated him in her farmhouse. Then she berated him verbally before beating the shit out of him with face slaps, punches, and a wooden stick.

The beatings would come to a head during a weekend in February of 2000. Sheila beat Kenny's face into a pulp, took the wooden cane to his legs and may have poisoned him.

Then she decided to take him shopping at Walmart.

Placing him in a wheelchair, she rolled him around the outlet as she stocked up on garden supplies. She dumped two containers of diesel fuel into the prone Kenny's lap.

Little did he know that she would later use the gas to incinerate his body.

Customers gawked at the odd couple, concerned about the contusions on Kenny's face.

"Fuck you looking at?" Sheila would scream as she sped down through the aisle.

Employees of the store soon became concerned, calling the police.

The cops would arrive, confronting the couple in the store. They inquired about Kenny's condition but he didn't respond. Instead, Sheila took the lead, telling Kenny that he "didn't have to talk to these assholes."

The police didn't follow through. Kenny remained silent as Sheila rolled him through the store and out the door. No crime had been witnessed and they let the couple go.

Kenny's mother would later sue the police for negligence but it was tossed out of court in 2010.

A few nights after the Walmart incident, Sheila would make a frantic phone call to the police.

"I got a pervert in my house!" she screamed into the phone. "He's a pedophile! A pedophile!"

In a bizarre sequence of events, Sheila began to play a recording for the detective on the other end. She had routinely audio recorded everything she did, trying to incriminate the young men she worked with into admitting they were pedophiles. On this occasion, she played back a recording of her and Kenny.

"On the tape was my son, vomiting," Lodge said. "He kept saying 'he's faking, he's faking.'"

Sheila would ask Kenny if he was a pedophile on the tape. Kenny would answer 'yes'.

"Now he's a pedophile," Kenny's mother said. "Now he's raping children. Raping his brother. He's vomiting."

The police would write off the call as the rantings of a schizophrenic. They did not immediately respond to the residence.

Sheila would then kill Kenny Countie.

"She had to justify the killing of the young men in her own mind," Orange said. "For some bizarre reason, she would brainwash herself into thinking that her victims were pedophiles. She would repeat the question like a mantra, 'Are you a pedophile? Are you a pedophile?' Working herself up into an angry and violent state of mind before she killed the man."

Sheila's sister, Lynn Noojin, believed that Sheila was sexually abused by her father. Because of this, she became obsessed with child molestation. She would accuse the young men that worked for her of various sexual deviations, including pedophilia, incest, and bestiality.

CHAPTER SIX

After the bizarre call to police, authorities would not arrive at the farmhouse until the next morning. The police would enter the grounds, seeing both the burning mattress and barrel with Kenny's remains. They would not identify the burning bones as belonging to Kenny until much later.

Sheila had murdered Kenny the night before. She attacked Kenny ferociously with a kitchen knife, pushing the already weakened young man to the floor and stabbing away.

Blood sprayed and splattered everywhere.

Sheila then dragged Kenny's body out to her yard where she doused his body with the diesel fuel they had purchased at Walmart.

Lighting a match, she set the dead man on fire. She then took her pet rabbit in her lap, pulled up a chair and watched Kenny Countie burn.

"He was dismembered," Kenny's mother said, fighting tears. "And he was put in a pit and burned. But my son, he just wanted to be loved. I can't imagine what he must have been thinking. Because he was all alone."

Police would look throughout the house and find blood splatter on the walls and floor. A forensic team arrived and matched the blood with Kenny's DNA sample from his Army days. They would find the wallet of Michael Deloge but not his body.

Hundreds of police would spend seventeen days searching the 115-acre property. They found numerous burn pits and blood remains that were so old they had layers of dust on them. They would find clothing that belonged to Deloge and some toes that remain unidentified (it is rumored that the toes may belong to a mysterious Irish man who Sheila claims was stalking her.)

Going on the run from the cops, Sheila hitchhiked along Interstate 293. She was then picked up by Stephen Martello.

"Thanks so much for stopping," Sheila said.

"No problem," Martello said, looking the buxom Southern Belle up and down. His heart began to race.

Will he get lucky?

"My car broke down about two miles back. I got into a fight with my boyfriend and I'm trying to get to Dorchester."

"I'm headed that way," Martello said.

Sheila clutched her purse as if it were a security blanket and she kept looking back at the rear window.

"You all right?" he asked.

"Yeah," Sheila said "Just a little rattled. You know, it has been a tough day."

Martello took Sheila to the drug store when she said she needed to stop off and "buy some things". He tailed Sheila around the store until she bought a douche. Noting her erratic behavior, Martello disappeared out of Sheila's earshot to call the police on his cell phone.

"Hi," Martello said. "Just curious if you folks are looking for someone who just robbed a bank or an escaped mental patient. I just met a woman who is acting kind of strange."

When the authorities informed him that they were not actively investigating someone with that kind of background, Martello took Sheila to a hotel room.

The two would engage in wild and loud sex.

"You just had sex with an angel," Sheila proclaimed after they were done.

"Is that right?"

"You're not like the other men," Sheila said. "My boyfriend, Jesus, I just caught him with a huge stack of child porn. He is a pedophile. So are all those damn cops. Pedophiles, all of them. I think all sex offenders must die."

Martello said nothing. Instead, he put his pants and shoes on as fast as he could as Sheila continued to go on another bizarre rant.

"Vengeance is mine saith the Lord," Sheila said,laying on the bed in post-coital repose. "I was sent back to earth as an angel. I know how to speak to God in Hebrew. Do it every night."

Martello excused himself and high-tailed it out of the hotel room. He arrived home and saw the television broadcast about Sheila. He didn't call the police, worried that he would be an accessory to her crimes. Instead, Martello drove to the station and practically sprinted to the front desk.

"I think I just met Sheila LaBarre."

"To the end, Sheila had control over just about every man put in front of her," Orange said. "Here was a guy who picks her up at the side of the road. He thinks she is crazy enough to where he calls the cops to find out if there are any missing mental patients. He knows that she has a screw loose but he has sex with her anyway. It may be a poor reflection on men for sure but his response is typical. The men that Sheila encountered, from Dr. LaBarre all the way to Stephen Martello, all had the same false narratives going on in their head. They did not see a beautiful woman as something evil. It just didn't fit their narrative. So when Sheila begins her abuse, they just can't believe it. They refuse to hit a 'woman' back. She gets them 'pussy whipped' then beats the shit out of them. Rinse and repeat."

Sheila LaBarre would later be arrested for the murders of Michael Deloge and Kenneth Countje. She would plead no guilty on the grounds of insanity.

"This is a sick, sick woman," her attorney would argue. "Deeply disturbed."

Court-appointed psychiatrists would agree, testifying that Sheila was delusional as well as schizophrenic.

The jury would visit both LaBarre's farm and the Walmart where she frequented first hand. Sheila would join them as well although she was forced to wear a stun belt.

The jury did not buy her insanity defense and found her guilty.

"The fact that she has to remain for the rest of her life behind bars," Kenny's mother said. "She got what she asked for. She'll never see the light of day. Horrible thing is that my son, he's not here with me. He was only twenty-four."

Sheila LaBarre is now serving life in prison without possibility of parole.

HUSBAND KILLER JANE DOROTIK

ANNA MICHAELS

Murder at the Charisma Ranch

Robert Dorotik was born in 1945, two years before his future wife Jane Marguerite Colvey. It would be 23 years before they would meet and fall in love. They married on April 4, 1970 in Los Angeles California.

Two years later Nicholas was born, another son Alexander would follow shortly after that and by January 16, 1976 their family would be complete with the birth of their daughter Claire Elizabeth.

Robert was an Engineer and Jane was a Health care professional as well as a successful business woman. She made a six figure salary from her 9-5 job alone, and the horse ranch she ran with her daughter was starting to bring in money too.

Robert and Jane would have more than one argument over the money Jane and their daughter Claire spent on Charisma Ranch. He quit his job as an engineer to support Jane's endeavor of raising and training horses. Bob started a business making horse jumps, but by 2000 his business was in trouble. One of the last arguments Jane and Bob had was when Jane and Claire told him they found another horse that would be perfect for the ranch. Robert complained they didn't need any more horses. This infuriated Jane and she told him in no uncertain terms that it was her money and she would spend it how she wanted, she didn't need his permission.

On the afternoon of February 13, 2000 Jane got ready to go down to tend to the horses. Bob was dressing in his jogging clothes and told Jane he was going to go for a run. Bob had been a long distance runner for years. Jane had an injury that prevented her from participating. Jane asked her husband to stoke the fire before he left and she went to the barn.

Mrs. Dorotik returned to the house a couple hours later and Bob was nowhere to be found. She waited a while longer and began looking for him. There were others including neighbors and sons Nick and Alex. Becoming increasingly worried about her husband Jane called the police and told them that he had not come home after his run. A search was organized by the police and in the early morning hours of February 14, 2000 Police found Robert's battered, bloodied body by the side of the road about three miles from home. Police immediately suspected Jane.

Robert Dorotik had died from blunt force trauma and strangulation. He had several injuries to the face and the back of the head (an expert testified the wounds were consistent with a hammer). There were defensive wounds on his hands. He was still wearing his jogging clothes although according to the detectives his shoes were tied in an odd manner. The rope used to strangle him was still around his neck and had made a laceration on his throat.

They did not find blood at the scene that would have been consistent with it being the murder site. Robert had been killed somewhere else and moved here. They found the tire tracks and shoe prints. Jane could not be linked to any of the shoe prints, only the tire tracks. However, hers were not the only tire tracks there, the others were not linked to anyone.

The evidence from the beginning seemed to point at Jane Dorotik as the killer. At the scene where they found the body there were tire tracks that matched the three different treads on her truck. At the residence there was a massive amount of blood that had been cleaned at. Jane claims that the blood was from a nosebleed Robert had and cleaned up. Between the box springs and mattress there was a towel soaked with blood. In a bag in the master bedroom they found a syringe with a horse tranquilizer in it and Jane's fingerprint in Bob's blood was found on it. She was arrested before the blood analysis could even be returned.

Around the room investigators found impact blood spatter patterns as well as drip, transfer and cast off. In one of the closets in the house they found a steam carpet shampooer and a significant amount of cleaning supplies. Bob's blood was found on the cap, handle and nozzle of one of the bottles.

Blood stains consistent with Robert's were found in the bed of the truck Jane, Claire and the ranch hands used around the ranch. They found no blood spatter on his shoes or shirt, but did find some blood on his boxers. One of the two hands never showed up for work the day after Bob's death.

Jane was booked into San Diego County Jail and with the help of family made bail.

Jane's daughter Claire was incriminated in the murder, that she was actually the one that killed Robert, her own father. It was well known that father and daughter had a stormy relationship, and at times became volatile. It was never revealed why the two seemed to hate each other, but Claire even wrote a scathing letter to her father about a "betrayal of trust."

Jane's defense team Kerry Steigerwalt and Cole Casey now had to figure out how to defend their 55 year old client. What they decided on wasn't the most unusual way to do it and it and many other attorneys had done in numerous courtrooms around the country. They deliberately brought Claire up as a suspect. By showing that another person 'could' have committed the murder there is a chance that it will raise enough of a doubt in a jury's mind for them to bring back an acquittal instead of a guilty verdict. This is what the attorney's for Jane were doing, trying to raise a reasonable doubt. This strategy would ultimately tear the family apart. In a letter written three years after her conviction Jane would call her attorney 'ego driven' and the implicating of her daughter a 'seriously flawed defense strategy.'

Prosecutor Bonnie Howard-Regan was convinced that Jane killed her husband to keep from having to pay him spousal support. It seemed there was an impending divorce on the horizon for Bob and Jane. They had separated in 1997 but talked it out and decided to keep their money separate and got back together.

Their own sons commented that their parents' marriage wasn't the most loving and at times their fights became very heated. But is this a motive for murder? Perhaps not just the fights, maybe it was the fact that if the two divorced Jane would have to pay Robert up to 40% of her annual income. This would be upwards of 50,000 dollars a year. Jane was incensed when a divorce attorney had told her that. That is a huge motive for murder in the eyes of the law. There was also a $250,000 life insurance policy on both Bob and Jane. She was forthcoming with the detectives about this during the investigation. If she had to pay that much out in spousal support she wouldn't be able to keep the horse ranch, and it seemed that was all she cared about.

Jane's trial would begin in May of 2001 a little over a year after her husband was murdered. Jane had pled not guilty and was making passionate pleas to the public declaring her innocence. Though her daughter and sister also claimed that Jane was innocent of this heinous crime, Claire, Bonnie Long and a ranch hand all invoked their Fifth Amendment right against self-incrimination. Steigerwalt brought up the fact that Claire's alibi was never confirmed. Had the Sheriff's Department zeroed in on Jane in a hasty attempt to close the case?

On June 9, 2001 the case of Jane Dorotik v The State of California went to the jury for deliberation. After the third day both the defense and the prosecution were starting to worry. Maybe they hadn't presented their case as well as they'd thought. Maybe they didn't explain things in an easy to understand way. In the end however, it wasn't that the jury had a problem understanding what they saw and heard during the trial. They were just being diligent, making sure every juror understood what the evidence was and how it fit in the scheme of things. In fact, they had a unanimous decision on the first vote...guilty on the charge of first degree murder.

Judge Joan Weber said that there was "an overwhelming amount of circumstantial evidence" and when Jane's attorney filed for a new trial it was denied. New witnesses had come forward and Steigerwalt asked that the case be reopened to the jury could hear what they had to say. She denied his request. Weber also asked, "How could you have your husband's blood on your hands if you had nothing to do with his death?" The Judge Weber was referring to the syringe with Janes fingerprint on it. It was an integral piece of evidence in the case.

Without a new trial in San Diego County, the next step is Court Of Appeal Of California, Fourth Appellate District, Division One.

The Court of Appeals works differently than the Trial Court. It is not a place for a new trial or a retrial. They won't look at new evidence or hear from new witnesses. It is strictly for trying to overturn the lower court's decision. If this happens then the Trial Court would be made to do one of several different actions in the case. One would be a whole new trial, which in Jane's case is what her attorney would want to happen. Or perhaps the Appellate Court would order Trial Court to look at additional evidence and/or revisit the facts in the case.

Either of these would be a win for Jane and her defense team. However, before these could happen her attorney would have to show that there was an error in the trial procedure or in how Weber interpreted the law.

This all starts with a Notice to Appeal, and then a brief has to be filed. In many cases appeals are decided based solely on this brief. Other times there will oral arguments before anything is decided.

Janes appeal was filed on November 18, 2003. She is asserting that Judge Weber should have included in the instructions to the jury the lessor charge of voluntary manslaughter because the state didn't present evidence that there was premeditation and aforethought to constitute first degree murder. She was denied.

On June 12, 2009 Jane filed another appeal. There were three key facts in this appeal. In the first one she claims 'ineffective assistance of counsel'. Jane claimed that her defense team didn't represent her properly. They didn't do any investigation of their own.

Second, she believed that not letting the jury hear from the new witnesses and not doing DNA testing jeopardized her case. The rope used to strangle Robert was never test for DNA, claiming that epithelia's of the real killer would have been found.

Third, there were procedural mistakes because of the delayed discovery and her actual innocence.

The defense was not allowed to present evidence that the State's expert witness had many mistakes in other cases by using 'faulty methodology'. The jury was not allowed to hear from an eyewitness.

The Appellate Court denied her, again.

The San Diego Union-Tribune reported on November 22, 2015 that a Judge has determined Jane be allowed to have the DNA in her case tested. The rope used to strangle Bob, the fingernail scrapings, and a piece of hair found around the victim's finger all be tested.

Jane still proclaims her innocence and said the ranch hand that didn't show up for work the day after the murder should be considered. He drives a black pick-up, and his tire tracks were also found at the scene. She also reiterated that the man owed the Dorotik's money.

Jane filed her first appeal on November 18, 2003. The Appellate court upheld the lower court's decision. Then Jane, known also as the petitioner filed Habeas petition on April 4, 2006 in the State Superior Court. Next was a Habeas Petition in the Appellate Court on January 3, 2006. And again Jane filed with the State Supreme Court on November 20, 2006. All appeals and motions to this point had been denied or affirmed the lower court's decision.

On June 1, 2007 Jane would file a Petition for Writ of Habeas Corpus, a Motion to appoint counsel, a Motion for Leave to Proceed in Forma Pauperis and a request for DNA testing. This too was denied or dismissed.

In July of 2007 Jane managed to get the money for filing fees and Magistrate Judge Porter ordered the case be reopened on July 9, 2007.

In the appeal for ineffectual assistance of counsel the superior court "denied the claims on the merits in a written order but only addressed the first two claims. On appeal the Appellate Court did the same thing.

Jane contends that council should have done independent testing of the forensic evidence that the prosecution would be presenting at trial and that there was other available evidence that he could have taken advantage of but didn't. Jane contends that had he done so the findings would have weakened the prosecution's case.

Another point the petitioner brought up is that her counsel didn't call her as a witness in her own defense.

Petitioner wanted a medical professional called as an expert witness to testify as to the medical impossibility that she could have perpetrated the murder due to an injury from an accident years earlier. That she would not have had the strength to do what the prosecution says she did.

Counsel for the defense did not object when a detective testified that he thought she was the killer. He could have also asked for a mistrial also.

He didn't insist on DNA testing prior to the start of the trial, armed with the results of the tests, petitioner is sure that it would have pointed to the real killer or killers.

Petitioner believes that her counsel should have brought up different scenarios that could have explained away the circumstantial evidence brought up at trial.

That he could have provided innocent theories for the incriminating evidence.

He didn't show that police didn't follow any leads, including eyewitnesses that came forward in the early stages of the investigation; they made up their mind that she was guilty. Therefore they didn't look for the real killer/killers.

Jane contends that her counsel could have done their own investigation and found the witnesses that were not heard at trial. Instead he made the leap to blaming Claire Dorotik as a defense.

And finally, follow through on the promises counsel made to the jury about what the evidence would show, and not make a comment to the affect that Jane was guilty.

If none of these ten points were true but the last one, would that fact that her own defense counsel made a comment that directly or indirectly told the jury he thought she was guilty should have been grounds for a mistrial and perhaps proceedings started to disbar her attorney.

The points brought up in Jane's eyes caused her to be wrongly convicted for the murder of her husband.

The forensic evidence in many parts does not support the prosecution's theory. Think about the "blood" found on the wall that supposedly dripped down from the master bedroom upstairs. The man who sold /rented the property to the Dorotik's knew of a water leak. Rain water would get in the track of the sliding door and seep down the wall of the stairs leading to the bedroom. There was Bob's DNA there, but was it from blood? Walking shirtless up the stairs and rubbing his sweaty arm on the wall could leave his DNA, it was not said that it was blood.

Post-conviction reports showed that there was way less blood present than would have been if the State's expert witness, Merrit, were correct. McDonell who did the post-conviction report says the fatal blow probably occurred outside the bedroom. But at the same time doesn't accept the idea that Bob was killed where he was found or that he was killed somewhere else, body dumped where it was found and the blood evidence planted.

McDonell also said that the blood on the mattress could have easily been caused by a bloody nose. That being said it still doesn't explain the different blood stain patterns found throughout the room. Those where found on the pillow, nightstand, walls, bedspread and the window. Those he said cannot be explained away by a nosebleed.

The post-conviction report says that Merrit's testimony was wrong inasmuch as there was not enough blood soaked in to support his idea that Bob remained on the mattress for a long time after the attack.

McDonell concurs with petitioner that the blood around the pot-belly stove could very well have been from the nosebleed. Petitioner wants further testing to find out if it even had anything to do with the murder at all.

The bloody thumb print on the syringe was due to Bob helping Jane with a vet procedure. There was a horse tranquilizer inside the syringe and Jane's thumbprint in Bob's blood on it. This was admitted into evidence? Why, it's said to be a 'key piece' of evidence in the prosecution's case. Petitioner's counsel didn't object? Per Bob's toxicology report there was no drugs in his system. How did they tie it into the murder?

The truck, tire tracks and shoe prints. There was much to do about the tire tracks at the scene where Bob's body was found. There were actually two sets, one belonging to the family truck, the one that everyone including the farm hands had access to. But there was another set, never identified. The shoe prints found also at the scene couldn't be attributed to Jane either. Both sets were too big. The tracks that showed Jane's truck had backed up at the spot where the body was found can easily be explained as well. Bob used the truck to measure jogging routes. If he were to come to the exact length he wanted, he would have just turned around at that spot, hence the backup tracks.

A cursory search of the house was done the evening that Jane reported Bob missing. Police and Police dogs were all in the house including the master bedroom. They didn't find any blood.

Jane was in an accident in 1983 and had a severe injury to a hip which had to be put back together with metal and screws. The prosecution says that Jane would have bludgeoned her husband, then carried him down the stairs from the bedroom, through the house, across a 60' porch and lifted him into the back of a full sized Ford

F250. Defense counsel should have brought up the fact that his client couldn't have done any of that. The Appellate court says that her sons saw her pulling irrigation pipes around the ranch that weighed about 75 lbs. pulling on 75lbs of something is different than lifting 147 lbs of dead weight.

Detective Richard Empson when questioned about the rope used to strangle Robert Dorotik and why it wasn't tested for DNA said the "criminologists in his office discouraged testing it because too many people had handled it." When pressed about the possibility of DNA on it that could have belonged to Claire or the ranch hand Leonel Morales or someone else and lead to the real killer, what then? Empson continued, "I believe I know who killed Bob Dorotik, that's why I arrested Jane Dorotik." Personal opinions are not supposed to be brought in to testimony, especially from an officer of the court. Did Jane's counsel object to this? Did it prejudice the jury against the petitioner? It could be said that it inflamed the jury. Most jurors will believe a law enforcement officer over anyone else. Even if the comment was objected to and stricken from the record the juror's still heard it and no matter if they are told to disregard it, it will still be in their mind.

There are so many points that Jane brought up on each one of her appeals. And each and every one of them were dismissed by the Courts. Many of Jane's friends and family still believe that Jane is innocent and should at least get a new trial so all of the evidence can be heard and that maybe she can even testify in her own defense. Although her trial court attorney believed that doing so was not a good idea. Clearly he didn't believe his client was innocent of the crime.

In the findings of the Appellate Court they say that the petitioner didn't show how not having the jury hear that Merrit's methodology was flawed and that he had been wrong on other cases would not have changed the jury's verdict.

They stated that even though the petitioner believes that the prosecution purposefully did not test for DNA she cannot prove how it would have changed anything. Also added the testing would not have brought forth any exculpatory or impeaching evidence. Knowing that DNA has set wrongfully convicted people free by proving their innocence this statement seems wrong in its entirety. Jane would be in a Catch 22 scenario, she can't prove that by not testing there was an error in law and without being able to prove it would help her case they wouldn't allow the testing.

Jane says she's been through a living hell since being sent to Chowchilla's prison facility in central California. But she hasn't been wasting her time. Along with filing the above mentioned appeals she is fighting for her fellow prisoners who are over the age of 55.

Jane is appalled at how many women are incarcerated and how the number keeps growing every year. She was once a mental health professional and says that a large number of women in prison should be in a Mental Health facility.

According to Jane "Medical care is liken to a third world country." And "there are women dying in prison alone and unnoticed by prison staff.

What she is trying to get done is this, have more compassionate releases, the parole board has the authority to do this but won't. So a program is working its way through legislation in the state of California. "If The Risk Is Low, Let Them Go".

Jane isn't advocating opening the flood gates and letting these women head off to parts unknown. There are a certain set of criteria in place to make sure the risk is actually low.

First of all, they have to have served at least 50% of their sentence or seven years.

They can't have had any disciplinary actions in the past five years. In other words they have to be a model prisoner.

They cannot have any other felony convictions of their record and they must have a concrete, safe place to stay in the community

These are safeguards to keep reoffenders inside the prison walls. Jane is very passionate about this program. She has watched many of what she calls "Golden Girls" languishing with terminal illnesses for years, alone, not able to be with family because Chowchilla houses inmates from all over the state.

Many of the families just don't have the money or time to be able to travel to see their loved ones. And even the children have to be patted down before they can go in to see a relative, to possibly say a last goodbye.

Jane's alternative custody program has to clear through law makers and with the help of different advocates it's headed in the right direction thanks to Carol Lui a senator from California.

This is being heralded as a great program to help with overcrowding of the prisons in California, and if this comes about in a timely manner it could help Jane as well. She is now 68 years old.

HUSBAND KILLER : THE TRUE STORY OF WENDI ANDRIANO

94

OLIVIA WATSON

Chapter 1

A dying husband needs a devoted wife. But when love runs out, marriage becomes a burden.

On October 8, 2000, Wendi Andriano snapped. She had played the part of devoted wife to her terminally ill husband, Joe Andriano, for years, but when the love left their marriage, so did Wendi's patience for her husband's eventual demise.

Wendi had a plan to help nudge nature along, and when her plan b expired, she took matters directly into her own hands and bludgeoned him to death.

Wendi first tried to poison her husband by spiking his last meal, a homemade beef stew, with sodium azide, but Joe Andriano did not ingest enough to kill him, only enough to vomit it back up. Wendi then grabbed the nearest object, a bar stool, and beat her dying husband over the head so many times that parts of his brain became exposed.

After thinking she had successfully killed her husband twice, Wendi then realized that Joe was still breathing, so she took a knife from the family kitchen and stabbed him in the side of the throat.

Minutes later, Joe was finally dead.

This bizarre and frantic way Wendi killed her husband isn't the strangest thing about the case though. Known even to Wendi, Joe was due to die from terminal cancer within the next few years anyways.

Why Wendi couldn't wait to kill her husband is an intriguing tale wrought with sex, lies, and strangely, a lack of patience.

Chapter 2

Wendi and Joe Andriano grew up together in the small farming community of Casa Grande, Arizona. But while they both had gone to the same school, they never dated. As a minister's daughter, Wendi's social life was restricted to her father's church. Her celebration for graduating high school was even in the form of a missionary trip to Mexico in 1989. When she returned she took a job at the local clerical hospital.

Wendi met Joe in 1992 through friends. Although when the couple started dating Joe's family found the minister's daughter to be an unusual fit for the loud, outgoing former football player, they all thought she was friendly enough and approved of the match.

Joe worked for a local boat builder. He was very mechanically inclined and was a very good welder. He owned his own boat and took Wendi for several cruises around the local hot spots for speedboats. They were inseparable.

The couple married in January of 1994. Their wedding took place in a baptist church across the street from their shared elementary school. Their reception was at the Elk's club and was populated by their many friends and family. Even after two years of dating, though, Joe's family felt like they didn't know his new bride very well, but Joe seemed to be very happy, so they were happy for him.

Soon after marrying, the couple became business partners when they started a small company that did windshield repair and replacement. The business combined Wendi's office experience with Joe's mechanical experience, skills they both exceeded at, and the business thrived.

The couple hadn't been married a whole year yet before they faced their first major challenge together. That fall, Joe noticed an odd bump on his neck. When he had it tested, he was told it was a non-cancerous benign tumor, but it wasn't long before they were second-guessing the diagnoses. A year after it was removed, the tumor grew back.

A second surgery and round of tests seemed to reconfirm that the tumor was benign, but shortly after Wendi gave birth to a son in 1997, the tumor was back yet again.

The third time the tumor returned, Joe's wife and family were convinced that the tumor had to be cancer. This fear was confirmed in 1998 when Joe underwent surgery to have the bump removed for the fourth time. Joe's pre-surgery chest x-ray showed that not only was the tumor cancerous, but that the cancer had now spread across Joe's throat, chest, and lungs.

The prognosis wasn't good—Joe had a rare form of cancer and while radiation and chemotherapy were standard, there was no guarantee they would work. On top of this, Wendi was also pregnant again and was only months away from giving birth to the couple's second child.

Chapter 3

In an effort to increase Joe's chances of survival while decreasing his suffering, Wendi and Joe decided to pursue holistic treatments before resorting to chemotherapy and radiation. They had been told that chemotherapy and radiation treatments would likely not cure Joe, but they would lengthen his life by a few years; however, these years would be anything from pleasant. The horrific side-effects chemotherapy and radiation treatments cause are well known.

So the Andriano's decided first to try anything from special diets to alternative medical treatments to prayer—anything that had a chance to help Joe. Joe even attended a holistic treatment centre for cancer patients in Colorado for a few weeks where he was surrounded by other men and women facing the same prognosis as him. After seeing the bravery of others in the same position as him, Joe began thinking about his future again and began to see it as bright for the first time in a while.

After Joe returned from his holistic healing getaway with a bright new attitude, the Andriano's decided the next best step would be for Joe to begin chemotherapy treatments. He had begun to crave his future and was ready to take steps to achieve it. Unfortunately, taking these steps meant that Joe needed to quit his welding job as well as his own position in the couple's business.

To help make ends meet, Wendi returned to working for the first time since the birth of the couple's children. She ended up taking multiple jobs and worked long hours while continuing to care for her husband at home. Eventually, Wendi landed a job managing the San

Riva apartment complex in the Ahwatukee foothills, an upscale neighbourhood outside of Phoenix.

Wendi's new job came with some major perks—the salary was above average, which was nice as Wendi was now the family's breadwinner, and it required Wendi to live on site, which meant that the family now lived in a luxury apartment but paid no rent. Wendi's new job also gave her a new life. A large part of her duties as complex manager was arranging social activities for the other residents of the San Riva apartments, who were mostly young, wealthy, single businesspeople.

Every Saturday the complex hosted picnics, pool parties, or late-night socials. The residents even had their own baseball team. Wendi was required to attend every event, which meant Joe was needed to stay home with their two children. Wendi enjoyed this alone time so much that many of the residents at the San Riva had no clue she had a dying husband and two children at home. She partied like she was single.

The first few months at the San Riva went well. Wendi organized mixers and pool parties for the tenants while Joe took care of the kids. Despite being very weak from treatments, he did everything he could, he wanted to do it. He prefered to have his kids around him even when he didn't feel good.

Although they had never gotten close to their daughter-in-law, Joe's parents also pitched in with babysitting so the couple could have time alone together. They didn't get to see each other much as Wendi began spending more and more time at work. Her new job had also given her a new confidence, and she spent many nights out on the town dancing and drinking away her weekday stress with friends. Joe began to fear that Wendi would soon leave him for her new lifestyle, but this fear got sidetracked when his health continued to fail.

In the summer of 2000, when tests revealed his cancer had spread yet again, Joe and Wendi decided to increase the frequency of Joe's chemotherapy. Joe agreed to undergo more treatments, but they quickly took their toll. He lost 15 pounds in the first week alone, and Joe's doctor became concerned. It went from bad to worse very quickly.

By the beginning of October 2000, it became harder and harder to remain optimistic about Joe's chances of beating his cancer. It became apparent it was terminal, but doctors insisted that with treatment Joe could live for several more years.

No one had any idea that Joe would be dead after only the first week of the month. No one, that is, except for one person—Wendi Andriano.

Chapter 4

Just after 2:00 a.m. on October 8, Wendi Andriano called a friend who also lived in the San Riva apartment complex. She told her friend that she needed someone to stay with the kids while she took Joe to the hospital. When the friend arrived, she found Joe on the floor, barely alive.

Joe was on the floor in the fetal position. There was vomit on the floor around him and he couldn't stand up. Wendi confided in her friend that she told Joe that she had called 9-1-1 and paramedics were on the way, but this wasn't true. After seeing Joe in such poor condition, the neighbour urged Wendi to call paramedics. She then went outside to wait for them to arrive while Wendi waiting with her husband.

Wendi did call 9-1-1, but when the EMT's arrived minutes later, she refused to let them or her friend inside the apartment. She said that her husband was dying from terminal cancer and had a do not resuscitate order. Joe was not to receive any medical attention.

Just over an hour later, at 3:30 a.m., Wendi dialed 9-1-1 a second time. The same team of paramedics came to the house. It didn't take them long to realize something wasn't quite right, so they contacted the police department. Both the paramedics and the police were shocked to find out that Joe, who had been terminally ill from cancer for quite some time had died, but not from the cancer that had been slowly killing his body. He died from being repeatedly beaten with a bar stool and from being stabbed in the neck.

When the police opened the front door of the apartment, they were confronted with obvious signs of a deadly struggle. The apartment was in a complete state of disarray, and there was blood everywhere. Blood had been traced throughout the kitchen, the dining room, and the living room of the luxury apartment, and blood had spattered across the walls the ceilings. Lying in the middle of the bloody scene was Joe, with a knife wound in his neck and holes spattered across his visible skull.

While crime scene technicians surveyed the apartment, phoenix police took Wendi down to the station for a formal statement. She was wearing clothes drenched in Joe's blood and was armed with a story that explained how Joe's death had been a complete accident.

In the interrogation room, Wendi told police she and joe had spent the evening in Casa Grande visiting with Joe's parents. They put the kids to bed after they returned home, which was when Joe noticed something odd about Wendi's appearance—she wasn't wearing her wedding ring.

According to Wendi, Joe worked himself into a rage and began accusing her of having an affair. This argument turned into a shoving match, and when Joe grabbed a belt, Wendi grabbed a bar stool and swung. Joe went down on all fours so she hit him again. It was then that she called her neighbour for help. Joe may have been in a terrible state when the neighbour saw him, but according to Wendi when she went outside Joe had gotten back to his feet easily.

Wendi said she denied the EMTs access to the apartment because she and Joe were both embarrassed about the fight, but just minutes after the EMTs left, the fight got physical again.

Wendi said that her husband tried to strangle her with a telephone cord and she defended herself with the first weapon she could get in her hands—a kitchen knife. She was vague about how the knife ended up in Joe's neck though, saying she was holding the knife up when Joe suddenly fell flat on his face. The next thing she knew, blood was spurting everywhere. He must have fallen on the blade, it was simply an accident.

Many things about this story didn't make sense to the police. First of all, the timeline presented in Wendi's story didn't match the accounts of Wendi's neighbour or the EMTs. Wendi's neighbour had seen no evidence of a physical fight when they first entered the apartment—there were no broken bar stools or blood like later when the police arrived. As well, Wendi had few injuries on her body, definitely no injuries that would necessitate self defence in the form of murder.

Joe's illness also shed doubt on Wendi's story. Joe's parents told police that when the Andriano's visited earlier that evening, Joe had been so weak from his treatments that he could barely stand. They had spent the evening doting on their sick son, bringing him any comforts he wanted. If he was too weak to stand, he certainly couldn't have been strong enough to violently attack Wendi.

Police also uncovered a damning piece of evidence from Wendi herself, in a moment when she thought she was all alone. The investigators that had been questioning Wendi left her on her own in the interrogation room for some time while they fact checked some of her statements and checked in with the investigators who were scanning the crime scene for evidence. During this time, Wendi made a phone call to a coworker at the apartment complex and asked them to hide some of her files from the police. This immediately led to a search of Wendi's office where police found evidence that Wendi had in fact killed her husband. She had even been planning it for months.

Chapter 5

While both investigators strongly believed that Wendi Andriano was responsible for Joe's death, they were stumped by her motive. Why would Wendi kill her dying husband? The police didn't know, but they did have one intriguing lead—the phone call Wendi had made from the interrogation room. They were determined to find out what she was trying to hide.

When they searched her office, police discovered that Wendi had been disciplined at work for using her computer to search inappropriate items on the internet while on the clock.She had been conducting research on poisons, and how to use certain poisons to kill people. They also discovered the papers that she had tried to hide—shipping notices for a substance known as sodium azide.

Sodium azide is a lethal substance with a variety of industrial uses including propelling airbags. It is not, however, something that the average person can simply go out and buy. It's not restricted to the point where only certain companies can possess it, but it needs to be bought for a reason—something that an apartment complex didn't have. But based on the information on the shipping invoice, Wendi had found a way around that.

Wendi had created a fictitious business license using the tax ID form for the apartment complex. Using a Xerox machine and an exacto knife, Wendi had removed all information specific to the apartment complex and inserted fictitious information for a fake company.

The business name on the shipping notice was bogus, but the address wasn't. Wendi had the substance delivered to an address in Scottsdale, Arizona in an attempt to distance herself, but that plan didn't work. When the police tracked down the real address on the invoice, workers at the company positively identified Wendi as the person who had come by a couple weeks earlier to pick up a package she had mistakenly had shipped there instead of her own office.

Wendi's coworkers had seen her with a package but that she had been very mysterious with the contents. She refused to tell anyone what was inside. Had this been the sodium azide? And if so, where was it now?

Chapter 6

Suspecting that Wendi had tried to poison Joe with the sodium azide, police took samples of every medication and food they could find in the Andriano's apartment. If Joe had ingested poison, it would have explained the awful state Wendi's friend had seen him in just over an hour before he died. Luckily, the remainders of Joe's last supper, homemade beef stew, still sat in a pot on the stove.

However, police didn't find any evidence of Wendi's mysterious package, or any evidence of the sodium azide itself in Wendi and Joe's apartment. They had just begun to lose hope in finding the poison when they found out Wendi had a storage space in the building that she failed to tell the police about. Hidden behind a stack of boxes in Wendi's storage unit was a small bottle of white powder and a measuring spoon. The white powder was soon identified as sodium azide.

But the storage unit wasn't the only place investigators found the lethal substance—it was also in Joe's stomach contents and in the beef stew on the stove.

While discovering the poison helped police understand that Wendi had been trying to kill her husband, it didn't explain why she had bludgeoned him to death on October 8, 2000. Wendi had spent a lot of time researching poisons and she spent a lot of time manufacturing documents so that she could purchase the poison. It certainly wasn't a spur of the moment decision.

But why would Wendi beat and stab her husband if she had already poisoned him? Prosecutors had a theory, one that would cut to the heart of the crime. It was patience—or more precisely, Wendi's lack of it—that had killed Joe in the end.

Wendi had grown tired of waiting for the cancer to kill Joe, so she decided to give nature a little nudge by poisoning his supper. But according to the theory, when Wendi gave Joe the poison, things didn't go quite to plan. Joe hadn't ingested enough poison to kill him when he began vomiting it back up. With her plan quickly failing, Wendi panicked. She snapped.

Now improvising, Wendi beat Joe with the nearest object she could get her hands on—a bar stool. Pathologists were able to conclude that Wendi beat Joe over the head with the stool no less than twenty-four times. This beating did render Joe unconscious, but still didn't kill him so Wendi grabbed a kitchen knife and stabbed him in the part of his body that caused all this trouble in the first place—the side of his neck.

Chapter 7

Ten days after she murdered her husband, Wendi Andriano was formally charged with first degree murder. Wendi's crime was viewed as being especially cruel due to the large amount of suffering Joe had had to endure over several hours thanks to Wendi's actions. Because of this, the prosecutor's on Wendi's trial did the almost unthinkable, they sought the death penalty.

When Wendi a walked into the Arizona courtroom on September 9, 2004 she looked vastly different from the perky apartment manager that the residents of the San Riva apartments used to know.

At the time of the killing she had been blonde, she had short hair, and generally appeared to be much younger and cute than the individual who appeared in court with long dark hair and thick glasses. Previously, she had liked to look good and show her figure so her conservative dress at the trial was certainly different from the look her friends were used to seeing. She was trying to look more conservative, more innocent.

She had had plenty of time to perfect her new look—it had taken prosecutors almost four years to bring the case to trial. It had been postponed about 12 times before it was finally brought before a judge and jury.

In their opening statement, prosecutors reminded the jury that at the time of the murder Wendi had been anything but the perfect mother or wife she claimed to have been. She had been someone who had no disregard for her husband at all. While her husband was dying, she had gone out partying and started affairs, and when his condition worsened, and it began to cramp her style, she turned to poison.

Wendi didn't like her new role as family breadwinner, especially with the loss of Joe's income, and with rising medical bills, the family was in the worst financial state they had ever been in. Wendi had thought she was going to be able to be a stay-at-home-mom for the rest of her life, and she did not adjust well to her return to the workforce. So Wendi had found an out.

Although Joe did not have any life insurance, even though Wendi had asked several friends to pretend to be Joe in medical exams so he could be insured, Joe had filed a malpractice suit against his former doctor who had continually told him his tumor was benign when it was in fact spreading throughout his body. If Joe died and the lawsuit went through, Wendi would likely walk away with a multi-million dollar settlement.

More than money though, Wendi had wanted freedom. She wanted the freedom to be single again, she wanted freedom to the ball-and-chain who was slowly dragging her spirit into his grave along with himself. Wendi wanted to not have to care about her dying husband anymore, who was too weak to provide her with any love.

Wendi maintained her plea of innocence throughout the trial, and her defence team attempted to prove she had been the victim of abuse not only on the night of Joe's death but also throughout the couple's entire marriage. To explain the poison, Wendi told the court that Joe had been the one who had grown tired of waiting for the cancer to end his life, and had asked Wendi to help him do it himself.

On the witness stand Wendi said that Joe had willingly taken the poison, but she also stuck by the story that she had originally told police, that Joe had suspected an affair and became enraged when she affirmed them. He became deranged and attacked her, starting the bloody fight. Wendi claimed Joe had died during the ensuing struggle.

Wendi's story wasn't enough to convince the court though, and on November 18, 2004 she was found guilty of the crime. It had taken the jury only two-and-a-half-hours to come to its unanimous decision. Six years after her husband joe had been diagnosed with terminal cancer, Wendi Andriano faced a possible death sentence of her own.

On December 20, 2004, the jurors assigned to Wendi Andriano's case met and decided on Wendi's fate—it would be death for Ms Andriano. Wendi, along with most of the courtroom, was aghast. Even Joe's family was shocked by the decision. Wendi Andriano became the second ever woman to be put on death row in Arizona, a state that reserves the death penalty for the worst of the worst.

Wendi Andriano has since attempted to appeal the court's decision, but as of early 2017, all attempts have been denied and Wendi continues to wait on death row. Wendi and Joe's children now live with Joe's parents, who continue to mourn the loss of their beloved son.

Joe Andriano's death was especially long, and especially cruel, but no happy ending was found when Wendi was sentenced to her own death. Many view the conclusion of this case to be the saddest possible outcome. On October 8, 2000, two lives were lost, and two children were left without parents.

THE SUNSET STRIP KILLER: The True Story of Carol Bundy

107

Jessi Gaines

Born Carol Mary Peters on August, 26, 1942, Carol Bundy's childhood, much like her adulthood, was spent pursuing a desperate need for attention and validation. Bundy's ability to idealize or overlook any unpleasantness made her a perfect victim for manipulators and abusers looking for a potential victim – a talent she picked up early on to deal with the abuses of her parents, Charles and Gladys Peters.

Bundy's memories of her childhood are happy ones – Christmases where her parents refused to let their three children miss out on the special holiday because of a lack of money, or her father's attempt to convince her that the tooth fairy had visited overnight, using a doll's feet to leave footprints through Bundy's bedroom. Bundy's mother worked as a hairdresser, but had previously been a stand-in for tap-dancer Ruby Keeler – and Bundy remembered her as a woman who exuded beauty and glamour.

Bundy, on the other hand, was awkward and unattractive, leading her mother to begin treating her as though she didn't even exist. When she was eight, Bundy came home to a locked door, and no matter how much she cried or begged her mother to let her in, Gladys refused – stating that Bundy was not her daughter. Eventually, Charles persuaded Gladys to let the girl in, but even though Bundy was allowed back into the home, her mother ignored her completely.

However, Charles was not without reproach. Gladys, who had a tendency to beat the children relentlessly with a belt, wasn't permitted to hit Bundy or her siblings – but Charles was fond of using physical abuse to assert his dominance. While Bundy remembers her father's beatings as fitting to the severity of the offense, Charles was an alcoholic who used Gladys' death as an excuse to move his assaults on his daughters from physical to sexual.

For eight months, Charles molested both Bundy and her sister Vicky, telling the girls it was their responsibility to "take their mother's place in his bed." Although Vicky maintains that the sexual abuse continued until Charles remarried, Bundy can only recall one instance where her father molested her – and described him as a good man, who loved her.

When Charles remarried, though, he began abusing Bundy more often – beating her, degrading her, humiliating her. He told her she was stupid and fat, and even that he wanted to kill her and the rest of the family – but he'd only gotten as far as the cat before his new wife had taken away his gun. After staying in foster homes, with their grandmother, and with an uncle, the girls were brought back to live with their father in California.

Desperate measures

At this point, Bundy was willing to do anything to get away from her father – and at the age of 17, she married a 56-year-old alcoholic to try and escape the abuse. Bundy had discovered how to use her sexuality and large breasts to seduce men and receive the attention she so desperately needed – but she was unwilling to prostitute herself for her new husband. When she left him, Bundy took up with another older man, a 32-year-old writer named Richard Geis.

With encouragement from Geis, who appreciated her wit and intelligence, Bundy embarked on a brief but somewhat successful writing career. However, after her father hung himself in 1962, Bundy sought comfort through sexual encounters with women. Bouncing frequently between male lovers and female lovers, Bundy was unable to find a reliable source of the attention she needed, so she eventually returned to Geis and the couple moved to Oregon.

Still, Bundy would occasionally let other men pay her for sex. Instead of urging her to seek counseling, Geis agreed to support Bundy while she attended nursing school in Santa Monica – he would pay for her education as long as she kept her grades up. In fact, Bundy was named class valedictorian when she completed the program in 1968.

It was in nursing school that Bundy met her next husband, Grant. Their relationship started off well, and continued to be relatively stable until the birth of their first son – but then, Bundy claimed, he started beating and belittling her. By the time Bundy had given birth to their second son, her eyesight had deteriorated to the point where it looked like she may have to give up nursing. Grant was faced with the prospect of being saddled with the responsibility of caring for a blind wife, as well as their two children, and grew increasingly more violent.

Bundy escaped the abusive marriage and took her two boys to a womens' shelter in 1979, where she stayed for two weeks before finding a small apartment in Van Nuys. The managers of the Valerio Gardens apartment building, Jeanette and John "Jack" Murray, took pity on the poor single mother, and Jack was frequently called on to help Bundy with issues at the apartment. Despite her husband's established pattern of cheating, Jeanette wasn't concerned about the 36-year-old month – Bundy was overweight with short brown hair, a stark contrast to Murray's typical blonde, long-legged mistresses.

The object of her affection

The kindness she saw from Murray led Bundy to develop a crush on her landlord, who took her to the Social Security office so she could receive disability payments and even to the optometrist, to get her fitted for a pair of glasses to help the single mother return to work. Murray, for his part, enjoyed having a captive audience. Good looking, with a fantastic voice, Murray had come to America from Australia to pursue a career in music – but had been unable to make it as a performer thanks to his arrogant attitude.

The two found exactly what they needed in each other, and soon began a sexual relationship. Bundy's crush rapidly became an obsession, and she started coming up with more frequent excuses to have her landlord visit her property. Her infatuation for Murray convinced Bundy that he was in love with her, too – even though he told her it would be years before he would be able to leave his wife. Bundy was well-versed in the art of overlooking negative or painful thoughts and feelings, and continued to look for ways to strengthen the connection she saw with Murray.

Regularly, Bundy loaned her landlord money and bought him expensive gifts after she received the settlement from the sale of the house she'd owned with Grant. She also opened a joint safety deposit box with Murray, and made deposits to help him cover the expenses he said he was incurring as a result of his wife's alleged cancer treatments. Still, Murray wasn't giving Bundy the attention she craved, and she started up a brief affair with Jeanette's younger brother.

In an attempt to spend some time alone with her lover, Bundy arranged a weekend for her and Murray in Las Vegas – as a "reward" for all of his help, she said. However, after the couple checked in at the hotel and took in a show, Murray left Bundy alone for the remainder of the weekend while he gambled. He returned in time to fly back with Bundy, and, hurt and upset, Bundy forgot her suitcase in Murray's van.

When Jeanette showed up at Bundy's door with the forgotten suitcase, Bundy used the opportunity to try and bring her affair with Murray to his wife's attention – thinking Murray would then be forced to leave his wife and finally be with Bundy. During their discussion, Bundy learned that Jeanette never had cancer, and she immediately confronted Murray. While Bundy was initially angry to learn that the money she'd given him to pay for the treatments had actually been used to pay off Murray's van, he calmed her down by reassuring her that his intention was still to leave his wife and eventually be with Bundy. Eventually.

However, Bundy was losing her patience. On Christmas Day, when Murray didn't show up to spend any time with her and her children, she made the decision to take matters into her own hands. Bundy attempted to bribe Jeanette into leaving her husband – which Jeanette accepted, as long as this was Murray's desire, as well. Bundy left with the hope that later that evening, she and Murray would finally be able to start their life together. But when Murray came to talk to her after discussing the situation with his wife, he told Bundy to "stay out of his life," telling her there was "no way" he would let her break up his family.

Devastated, Bundy spent a few days licking her wounds, but still turned up three days later at Murray's favorite bar, the "Little Nashville Club." Murray regularly played music at the bar, but that night, he was simply enjoying himself off-stage, dancing with his wife. Heartbroken, Bundy felt her dream of a life with Murray slip further and further away – but caught the eye of an attractive blond gentleman, who she saw watching her from across the bar.

After an evening of dancing, Bundy was taken with the stranger from the bar. Rather than taking advantage of her promiscuity, this new man treated Bundy with respect – which made her feel like a true lady, cherished and appreciated. Charmed, Bundy felt like she and Doug Clark were made for each other, and was already looking forward to seeing him again when he dropped her off at home and promised to call on her soon.

A whirlwind romance

Doug Clark waited only a few days before calling Bundy and asking to see her again. Although Bundy preferred to keep her male callers away from her children, she relented when Clark suggested he come over for dinner – and was pleased to see that her boys took to him immediately. They played, cuddled, and Clark even tucked the boys in for bed before telling them that he would be spending the night with their mother. Bundy loved the way he took care of things, and was more than willing to give him complete control.

For the first time, Bundy made love with a partner who seemed truly interested in giving her pleasure, rather than just letting her do all the work. He was an affectionate lover, telling her over and over again how much he wanted her, how much he appreciated her, how smart and beautiful she was. This was all new to Bundy, and played right into her desperate need for validation.

The next morning, however, Bundy awoke to see Clark looking concerned and anxious – his landlady was causing him grief, he said, so would she mind terribly if he moved some of his things into her apartment? Enamoured, Bundy was eager to accommodate Clark's desires, even when he requested a pair of her panties – just so he could remember her, even when they were apart. Although she felt somewhat uncomfortable with it, Bundy gave her new lover a pair of her large, cotton panties, which he promptly returned to her when he saw how big they were. Bundy was hurt, but she was still thrilled to have found such an attractive, caring, respectful man who was so interested in her.

Still, Clark's attentions weren't enough to tear Bundy away from Murray. After sending him several letters professing her deep, unwavering love for him, Bundy made another attempt to manipulate him away from his wife. This time, though, Murray refused to indulge Bundy's long-standing delusions, and told her it was finally time to move out of the building. Although reluctant, Bundy moved into a new apartment just three miles away – big enough for herself, her two sons, and her new lover.

After moving her furniture into the new suite, Murray left with his wife, but returned frequently to have sex with Bundy or persuade her into lending him more money. Not surprisingly, Murray and Clark disliked each other immediately, which Bundy interpreted as jealousy – a sign of their love for her. She told Clark how Murray had exploited her affection for him by asking for loans and gifts. Enraged, Clark demanded that Bundy cut him off immediately. She agreed, but kept the joint account open.

The perfect couple

Clark's anger over Murray's mistreatment of Bundy encouraged her enough to overlook the fact that her new live-in boyfriend wasn't covering his share of the rent, bills, or food. Bundy's new job at Valley Medical Centre, where she was now working as a vocational nurse, paid her more than enough to cover the expenses – and Bundy was content to take care of everything, as long as Clark continued to provide her with his love and affection.

Unfortunately, Clark was having a hard time keeping this up. He was proving himself to be just as self-absorbed as Murray – talking constantly about himself and his needs, with no real interest in hearing about anything Bundy brought up. However, the couple grew closer together after Clark read an article about expressing true love by fulfilling each other's fantasies. Eagerly, Clark convinced Bundy to start opening up about her own sexual desires, and he began to do the same.

Clark's fantasies were dark, but Bundy was thrilled that he was sharing these intimate thoughts with her. Bundy had a budding interest in bondage and domination, and particularly enjoyed imagining herself as Clark's captured sex slave – although in his fantasy, this role was filled by some young girl. But Clark loved that Bundy's sexual limits seemed virtually non-existent, and he pushed to include even darker subject matter, even murder. If she loved him, Clark told Bundy, she "should be willing to kill for him." Desperate to please him, she assured him that she would.

Their relationship was inconsistent. Clark would regularly disappear for hours and even days at a time, withdrawing from Bundy and drawing out her deepest insecurities. When he would eventually return, Bundy would be so relieved and happy to see him that she would say anything to convince him to stay. She also continued to react with pleasure and excitement as Clark's nighttime fantasy sharing grew increasingly sordid and graphic – even when he told her details of an ex-girlfriend's experiences with necrophilia.

A near escape

Bundy's penchant for promiscuity led her to browse personal ads occasionally, especially during Clark's frequent absences. When a posting from a well-to-do studio executive named Art Pollinger caught her eye, Bundy bravely responded to the ad. Pollinger weighed nearly four hundred pounds, but he was looking for a wife and thought Bundy a worthy prospect. Her tried-and-true method of using her past abuses to entice new lovers paid off again, and Pollinger – who genuinely enjoyed Bundy's company and thought her to be an intelligent and interesting woman – encouraged her to cut ties with Murray.

Eventually, after some persuading, Bundy allowed Polliger to drive her to the bank, where she withdrew the money she had left in the joint safety-deposit box she'd opened with Murray. Nearly $6000 was missing, and withdrawal slips were signed with Murray's name, but Bundy continued to defend Murray's deceit. Still, she took the rest of the money and put it in a chequing account where Murray would be unable to access it.

Despite Pollinger's genuine affection and desire to share his life with Bundy, the two ended up parting ways. Bundy was used to the emotional abuse she had endured in her previous relationships, and couldn't be satisfied in a healthy relationship.

Red flags

After having surgery to restore her sight, Bundy was excited at the prospect of purchasing a new car – and so was Clark, who had selected a blue 1973 Buick station wagon. Even though the car was large and difficult for Bundy to drive, since her peripheral vision was severely limited, she bought it anyway. She was desperate to give Clark everything he asked for – even guns, which he said she should have for protection. From a pawn shop in Van Nuys, Clark selected two .25 calibre Raven automatics, which Bundy was more than willing to pay for and register in her own name.

By now, Bundy's older son was starting to notice how Clark dominated his mother, and begged her to kick him out. Instead of taking her child's concern to heart, however, Bundy refused to acknowledge Clark's abuse – choosing to lash out at her son, instead. Clark and Bundy regularly beat him, and once, Clark even graphically detailed how he could kill the boy – with Bundy's son right next to him. Rather than defending her child, though, Bundy merely watched as Clark's behaviour grew more and more violent.

The couple had even stopped having sex, as Clark informed Bundy that she was too unattractive to arouse him anymore. Desperate to please him, Bundy began accompanying Clark as he picked up prostitutes from the Sunset Strip, and would watch from the backseat while he forced the usually young women to service him orally.

According to former FBI Special Agent Robert R. Hazelwood, who worked with the Behavioural Sciences Unit, men like Clark employ a specific process that can turn vulnerable women into accomplices. After identifying a woman like Bundy, desperate for attention, they use seduction techniques to reshape the woman's sexual norms – even if the woman is initially disturbed or frightened.

"These men have the ability to recognize vulnerable women and manipulate them," Hazelwood said. "The behaviour gets reinforced with attention and affection, gifts and excitement. Eventually, they are doing things that isolate them and further lower their self-esteem. All they have is this guy, so they cooperate."

Clark had plenty of experience in charming women enough to get them to do whatever he wanted, but although he had tried, he had been unable to find a suitable woman to replace Bundy. None of the other women he dated were as willing to indulge his dark sexual fantasies as Bundy was, so despite his mounting contempt for her, Clark continued to live with Bundy on and off. Bundy reassured herself that even though Clark had other girlfriends, she was the one he shared his intimate fantasies with – his feelings for her, she thought, must be deeper.

More than just fantasies

When Clark showed up at her apartment in late April, 1980, covered in blood, Bundy realized his murderous tendencies had taken a step beyond his imagination. Although Bundy chose to believe a fabricated tale Clark wove where he'd been attacked by a girl's boyfriend, the real story came out when a young prostitute named Charlene identified Doug Clark as the man who had stabbed her repeatedly with a knife after picking her up and requesting oral sex. She had been lucky to escape alive.

Bundy's suspicions mounted further when she discovered a bag of clothes and a blanket in the backseat of the Buick – covered in blood. When she confronted Clark, he told her the same kind of graphic story of sexual perversion that she'd become accustomed to hearing – only this time, the story was real.

Clark had spotted two young runaways, 15-year-old Cindy and her 16-year-old stepsister, Gina, at a bus stop. After picking them up and demanding Cindy give him oral sex, he told Bundy that he shot both girls until they were dead and then drove with the bodies to a garage he rented in Burbank. Once inside the garage, Clark said he dragged the bodies onto an old mattress and proceeded to perform acts of necrophilia on their corpses.

That night, after confessing to Bundy, Clark returned to the garage with a camera borrowed from one of his other girlfriends. After playing with the bodies again, he wrapped them in the blanket and dumped them in a ditch off the Ventura Freeway. Bundy was thrilled that he'd chosen to confess this activity to her, instead of any of the other women he was involved with.

Still, Bundy felt compelled to report the murders to the Van Nuys police. When she called the department the night after Clark's confession, she told the officer that she believed her boyfriend had committed the crime. Although Bundy told the officer some details of the case, she wasn't taken seriously, and when the call was disconnected, they assumed the "crank caller" had just hung up.

Clark started telling Bundy about other murders he claimed to have committed, including the killing of a man named Vic Weiss and the slaying of a young prostitute identified by police as teenage runaway Marnett Comer. Their relationship had become completely centered around Clark's murderous desires and Bundy's desperate need for his attention. Even though he no longer made any attempt to flatter or even be kind to Bundy, Clark had her completely under his control.

Only a few months later, at the end of June, Bundy accompanied Clark on what would be their first murder together. Cathy, who the couple picked up off Hollywood's Highland Avenue, looked about 17 years old, and agreed to perform oral sex on Clark for $30. Bundy, watching from the backseat, passed Clark the gun when Cathy failed to get him erect. He shot her, and as she lay dying with her head in Bundy's lap, Clark drove the car out into the country. Cathy was left along a gravel road near the Magic Mountain amusement park.

The very next night, Clark came home and told Bundy of another killing. He'd spotted three prostitutes working together, and convinced one of them, Exxie Wilson, to get in the Buick. After killing her and cutting off her head, Clark realized the other two women might be able to identify him if Wilson's body was found, so he went back and picked up one of the other prostitutes, later identified as Karen Jones. Clark left Jones' body near the Burbank Studios, and, after giving up on finding the third girl, returned to Bundy's apartment with Wilson's head.

They kept the head in the freezer for a few days, and Clark told Bundy how he would take it into the shower with him and push his penis into the open mouth. Eventually, Bundy cleaned the head and put it in an ornate treasure chest, which they dumped near the Studio City Sizzler where Clark had left the rest of Wilson's body. The chest was discovered almost immediately, and the relationship between Bundy and Clark grew even more strained.

The unraveling

In an attempt to gain back Clark's affections, Bundy agreed to participate in a three-way sexual relationship involving their 11-year-old neighbour, who Clark had been molesting for months. Since news of the Sunset Strip murders was spreading, prostitutes were hesitant to work alone, and it was increasingly difficult for Clark and Bundy to find anyone willing to get in their car.

Police were holding press conferences where they discussed evidence that seemed to link the cases – leading them to believe this may be the work of a serial killer. It was even suspected that the killer lived in the area, Detective Sergeant John Helvin stated to the press, "but we don't know for sure."

The stress of this ongoing investigation and Clark's lack of interest in her led Bundy to a desperate suicide attempt, and when she woke up alone at a hospital in Burbank, Bundy called Murray to come pick her up.

Bundy was willing to do anything to reignite Murray's sexual interest in her, so she started bringing her young neighbour for him to fondle. When that still wasn't enough, Bundy turned to her reliable method of playing the victim to gain her lover's sympathy – she told Murray about the murders. Although Murray didn't threaten to tell the police, Bundy knew she couldn't keep him alive. Besides, this was her opportunity to prove to Clark that she would kill for him.

On August 3, 1980, Murray climbed into the back of his van, anticipating oral sex. Instead, Bundy shot him in the head twice and stabbed him in the back half a dozen times. When she realized the bullets in Murray's head would help the police identify her gun, she cut his head off and put it in a plastic bag, eventually dumping it in a trash can near Griffith Park.

The rest of his body was found just days later, left in his van in the parking lot at the Little Nashville club. Police began questioning regulars at the club, including Murray's wife, Jeanette. Bundy was brought down to the police station and gave detectives her version of the alibi she had already discussed with Clark, which included a detailed description of a man she had supposedly sold her two guns to.

But none of this was enough for Clark, who refused to accept any of the blame for the rapidly deteriorating situation. He told Bundy that he was moving out, and left her alone while he went out to spend time with a new girlfriend. After briefly speaking to her mother-in-law and her sons, Bundy called Geis and told him about the murders. The next morning, after being berated by Clark as she drove him to work, Bundy confessed to a co-worker about the crime spree. By the end of the day, both Clark and Bundy were arrested in relation to the series of Sunset Strip murders.

According to police commander William Booth, evidence gathered during the investigation of Murray's death, along with the information collected during the ongoing investigation into the Sunset Strip murders, let them to Clark and Bundy. Bundy would end up telling the police graphic details about each murder, admitting that she thought killing was "really fun to do."

The end of the Sunset Strip

Despite the mountains of evidence connecting Clark to the killings, he continued to claim his innocence – even after he was found guilty on six counts of murder and sentenced to death. Bundy, who had initially entered a plea of "not guilty by reason of insanity," managed to avoid a similar fate by pleading guilty to her two counts of murder. She was sentenced to two consecutive terms of 25 years to life, with an added two years for using a firearm illegally.

Until her death in 2003, Bundy fought desperately to prove Clark's innocence – even as he attempted to put all the blame on her.

CYNTHIA COFFMAN

James Marlow and Cynthia Coffman were a troubled couple who were convicted of murdering five people during a deadly rampage that spanned multiple states. The last two victims, 20-year old Corrina Novis and 19-year old Lynell Murray were kidnapped and found strangled and sodomized, and the murderous pair were found guilty of the crimes. Whereas both Marlow and Coffman received the death penalty for Novis' death, Marlow received a second death sentence for Murray's while Coffman was sentence to life without the possibility of parole in Murray's murder. Both defendants sought to shift the onus of blame to the other with Marlow claiming it was Coffman's idea to kill the girls while he only wanted to rob them and Coffman alleging that she was the victim of battered women's syndrome. Neither ploy was successful as the pair were convicted across the board for robbery, kidnapping, sodomy, and murder. Coffman has the distinction of being the first woman sentenced to death in California following the state's reinstatement of the death penalty in 1977.

Early Lives

James

James Gregory Marlow was born on 11 May 1956 in Ohio but raised in Kentucky; the son of a beautiful but amoral hillbilly woman named Doris who virtually ensured that her son would grow up completely dysfunctional. Throughout his childhood, Marlow witnessed abuse, neglect, drug use, and sex courtesy of his mother who often prostituted herself in front of him. She gave birth to another child, Veronica Koppers, in 1959 and would frequently leave her children alone or with neighbors. Marlow eventually went to live with his father, Arnold, who would beat him severely and lock him in cabinets and, subsequently, went back to his mother's house. Despite the abuse and her horrific behavior, Marlow loved his mother dearly. So much, in fact, that when he was 13 years old his mother shot him up with drugs and seduced him. During interviews Marlow openly admitted to having had sexual relations with his mother on several occasions and that he didn't know it was wrong. He loved his mother so much and thought it was normal. Experts assert that Marlow suffered from traumatic bonding in which a traumatic event—his mother's seduction—created a dysfunctional yet significant bond from which he could not escape.

By the time Marlow was 16 years old he was living alone in California and married his first of three wives. Thanks to his mother, Marlow developed a severely skewed view of women. When she died in a trailer fire he was completely distraught and "took on the sins of his parents" by turning to a life of crime and violence. In one incident when he was still a teenager, Marlow was talking to one of his cousin's girlfriend, Darlene Miller, who he—one day while driving her to a nearby convenience store—pulled over in front of an old, abandoned house and forced Miller into the house where he beat and hogtied her, and then locked her in a closet. Over a span of three days Marlow would repeatedly beat, rape, and sodomize Miller. She escaped and ran to a neighbor's house—a house that Marlow had recently burglarized. Police were called and Marlow was arrested and after a tearful pretrial interview wherein he tearfully detailed the issues with his mother, he was sent to a drug rehabilitation center in 1975 for seven months and, soon after his release in 1976 was rearrested for being under the influence. Marlow was eventually imprisoned for burglary, robbery, and drug charges and was ultimately sentenced to California's notorious Folsom Prison in 1980. It was here that Marlow—not unlike the majority of inmates—got heavily tattooed with one—a howling wolf on his right side—earning him the nickname of the Folsom Wolf.

Prior to meeting Coffman, Marlow had an extensive criminal record. On 5 November 1979 in Upland, California, Marlow and his friend Allen Smallwood, who were both heroin addicts, assaulted Jeffrey Johnson in his apartment, searched it for non-existent drugs, then took Johnson downstairs—by knifepoint—to the Liesches' apartment where they searched the second apartment for more non-existent drugs, tied up the residents—Lori and Kathy—with electrical cords, and stole some cash they had found.

The following day, Marlow entered an Upland, California, leather goods store owned by Joanne Gilligan who was helping a customer, said he had a gun in his pocket and ordered them to lie on the floor, and then robbed the register of cash and took two jackets.

At approximately 10:00 a.m. on 20 November that same year, Gertrude Smith and Wilson Lee were working at an Ontario, California, methadone clinic when Marlow and Smallwood entered brandishing a sawed-off shotgun and pistol, respectively, and demanded methadone which they were told was locked in a safe. Another employee opened the safe and the two left with methadone that had a street value of $10,000. When Marlow was finally arrested on 26 November he had a bottle of methadone in his jacket and had the shotgun wrapped in a shirt.

Cynthia

Cynthia Lynn Haskins was born on 19 January 1962 in St. Louis, Missouri. From the beginning her life was to be difficult. Born with a double hernia that precluded her mother from holding her, Cynthia never experienced the necessary mother-infant bonding so crucial for healthy adjustment. As a result, she suffered from a crucial lack of empathy and a driving propensity to seek affections elsewhere. Cynthia's father left when she was three years old and her mother—who had aspirations of becoming a singer—allegedly tried to give her and her brothers Robbie and Jeff away several times during their childhood; with Jeff eventually given up for adoption. Cynthia was frequently "farmed out" to relatives that made her become more rebellious, defiant, and reckless. By the time she was a sophomore in high school, Cynthia was already experimenting with marijuana and methamphetamine with her new friends.

Her mother remarried a successful businessman named Bill Maender with whom Cynthia did not get along. Truancy, rebelliousness, and ultimately not wanting to live by her stepfather's rules caused Cynthia to run away at age 17 to her boyfriend's, Ron Coffman, house. When Cynthia returned three months later, pregnant, abortion was not an option for her devout parents and she refused to give the baby up for adoption, so she was forced into a loveless marriage with Coffman. The marriage quickly deteriorated and Ron filed for divorce because of Cynthia's infidelities, drug use, and poor housekeeping while Cynthia accused him of physical and emotional abuse and infidelity. Cynthia then worked in a carburetor factory to take care of her son, Joshua. She ultimately abandoned Joshua after two years, leaving him with her ex-husband (allegedly intending to get him back after she got settled) although later, when she and Marlow were committing their heinous crimes she suggested that Marlow kill her ex-husband and ex-in-laws (who had legal custody of Joshua) so she could regain custody of her son. While on death row Coffman exchanges letters with her son who believes his mother to be in prison for drug-related charges. She has stated in interviews that she wants to be the one to tell him the truth someday.

There is much speculation that Coffman had antisocial personality disorder which is characterized by little regard for right and wrong or the feelings of others. Further, those with the chronic disorder tend to manipulate, antagonize, and treat others with a callous indifference, are very prone to violate the law, are easily angered, lie, behave impulsively and/or violently, and use and abuse drugs and alcohol—all without remorse or guilt. Coffman exhibited a number of these traits, many of which worsened once she began her relationship with Marlow.

In May 1984 Coffman left home with a girlfriend and journeyed west where she wound up in Page, Arizona, and moved in with her new boyfriend, Doug Huntley. The lovebirds moved to Barstow, California where Huntley had some friends. He secured employment in construction while she was a bartender and waitress and sold methamphetamines on the side. One evening they were involved in an altercation outside of a convenience store in which Coffman pulled a gun on several men who were hassling her boyfriend and this resulted in both Huntley and Coffman being arrested and jailed. While Coffman was released after a few days, Huntley became cellmates with Marlow. Huntley told Marlow all about Coffman which intrigued Marlow who, upon his release soon thereafter, showed up at Coffman's apartment. It was love at first sight as Coffman reminded Marlow of his mother and Marlow was every bit the bad boy to whom Coffman was attracted. Even after Huntley was released, Marlow, Coffman, and he remained friends until Huntley returned to prison in June of that year.

A Dangerous Partnership

Marlow and Coffman began their contentious, dysfunctional, and murderous relationship amidst drugs and violence; her former boyfriend Huntley all but forgotten. In June 1986 Marlow had Coffman drive him to Fontana, California, and to his cousin Debbie Schwab's house where he purchased methamphetamines. A few days later they went to Newberry Springs and stayed with some of Marlow's friends, Steve and Karen Schmitt. Marlow told Coffman that he was a hit man, a martial arts expert, and a White supremacist who had murdered African American while in prison. It was during this time that Coffman saw Marlow turn into "Wolf"—his angry, violent alter-ego. Coffman testified in court that Marlow would beat her and then apologize and things would be fine again for a while. This is classic cycle-of-violence behavior central to most domestic violence cases. At this point Marlow allegedly took Coffman's address book that had her mother's and son's addresses and refused to give it back to her; essentially holding it as a carrot just out of reach to get her to do what he wanted.

They traveled across the country visiting Marlow's relatives in Kentucky and Tennessee. He had told Marlow that his father had recently died and left him some land in Kentucky and that they could get her son and live as a family there. First, however, they needed a vehicle and Marlow allegedly pressured Coffman to steal her friend's red Nissan pickup truck that Marlow and friend Paul Donner painted black. Marlow and Coffman jumped in the truck, stole some license plates from an off road vehicle outside of Newberry Springs, California, and headed east.

In Woodland Park, Colorado, Marlow called Gene Kelly, a contractor who constructed microwave telephone relay towers and who Marlow had met when he was a temporary laborer for him a few years back, to see if he needed any help in Colorado at the time. (There is some discrepancy in the available literature with respect to this individual being named Gene Kelly or Elmer Lutz; however, the actual criminal case against the defendants state Kelly). Kelly told him that he didn't have any work at the time but that he would have some work in Atlanta, Georgia, in a few weeks. The couple went to Colorado Springs for a couple of days and then to St. Louis to see Coffman's grandmother. They arrived on 2 July and Coffman called her mother who was less than happy to hear from her. The couple continued their journey east.

In Pine Knot, Kentucky, Marlow called his cousin Donald "Lardo" Lyons and both he and Coffman stayed with him for several days. Marlow had expected a modest inheritance from his grandmother Lena Walls with whom Marlow and his sister Veronica were close when they were younger; however, by the time Marlow reached Kentucky there was nothing left for him. Needing money, Marlow agreed to meet with Lardo's friend Shannon "Killer" Compton and the trio discussed how a local man named Greg "Wildman" Hill was going to be testifying in court against a mutual acquaintance and that Hill should "be silenced." They arranged for Compton to give Lyons a sum of money of which Lyons would give $5,000 to Marlow to get rid of Hill.

The next day, 7 July 1986, Lyons gave Marlow a .22 caliber pistol and at 5:00 a.m. Marlow and Coffman got into their stolen black Nissan pickup and drove to Hill's house. For most of the day the two of them parked relatively close and surveilled his house, did drugs, and engaged in sex. Finally, Marlow ordered Coffman to take off her shirt and bra and to tie a bandana across her chest like a bikini top and to knock on Hill's door to elicit help for her "stalled" truck. Hill agreed and tucked his own pistol inside his jeans' waistband. At the truck, when Marlow came after Hill with his own gun, Hill drew his and after an ensuing struggle Hill's gun went off, mortally wounding him with a bullet to the head. Marlow wiped his fingerprints off Hill's gun and left it at the scene.

Lyons kept true to his word giving Marlow the $5,000 "fee" for his "hit." The next day Marlow gave the stolen Nissan to a relative and spent $3,000 on a Harley Davidson; something he wanted for a very long time. On 11 July 1986 Marlow and Coffman had a "biker" wedding atop a Marlow's new Harley. Witnesses alleged that Coffman's face was bruised and scratched from a recent beating Marlow have given her. Such violence was not an isolated incident. In fact, one time while Marlow was assaulting Coffman one of his acquaintances asked what he was doing and Marlow dislocated his arm. As a result, nobody else ever intervened when Marlow was in one of his rages against Coffman. She said that when Marlow turns into "Wolf" his voice becomes monotone and his eyes and facial expression changes—that he becomes a completely different and violent person.

Marlow ended up giving the Nissan to a friend and purchasing a 1970's Cadillac to continue their journey to Atlanta and a job with Kelly. Marlow did manage to work for four days before an incident wherein he, Coffman, and a group of coworkers went out for dinner but which turned into Marlow beating Coffman outside of the restaurant and inside the vehicle, seemingly because she assisted some men with a stuck ball at a pool table. Back at the hotel where they were staying, Marlow was not finished with Coffman. He asked her for her scissors and then queried, "Your hair or your eye?" Horrified, Coffman said her hair and Marlow cut it as short as he could with her small scissors. He then taunted her that he would pierce her eye as well before making her strip naked and forcing her to stand outside the hotel room for several minutes. He then let her back into the room where he forcibly sodomized her. The following morning Marlow found a check from Kelly that had been slid under the door for his four days of work. After a few more days of going on "pot hunts" and unsuccessfully attempting a burglary in July 1986 in Whitley County, Kentucky, the couple left and headed back to Arizona.

In Arizona, Marlow and Coffman burglarized her former boyfriend Doug Huntley's parents' house and stole their safe that contained ten silver dollars—which they kept—and some papers. They buried the safe in the dessert. The next stop was back in Newberry Springs, California, where the couple stole two rings from the Schmitts; one they pawned for cash and the other they traded for methamphetamines.

Returning to Fontana, California, in early October 1986, Marlow and Coffman stayed with his cousins, the Schwabs. During their visit Marlow tattooed "Property of Folsom Wolf" on Coffman's buttocks and the word "W-O-L-F" and some lightning bolts on her ring finger as a wedding band. They then spent some time with Marlow's friends Rita Robbeloth and her son Curtis, and then with his sister, her husband Paul Koppers, and his brother, Steve. During this time Coffman alleges that after asking for an equal share of the methamphetamine they had, Marlow became angry and beat her, threatened to kill her, forced her to consume pills he said were cyanide, extinguished a cigarette on her face, and stabbed her in the leg. The pair then went to stay with another of Marlow's friends, Richard Drinkhouse.

The Crimes

On 11 October 1986 they were linked to the death of 32-year old Sandra Neary of Costa Mesa, California who never returned from a quick trip to a local ATM machine to withdraw some money. Her car was found in a nearby parking lot and her body was later found on 24 October by some hikers near Corona, California. Their next victim was 35-year old Pamela Simmons. She was reported missing in Bullhead City, Arizona, on 28 October. Her abandoned car was found by the local police department and the theory was that she was also abducted while withdrawing money from an ATM.

Corinna Novis

On 7 November, 20-year old Corinna Novis vanished from a First Interstate Bank parking lot near a shopping mall in Redlands, California, in broad daylight. Alone, she was driving her white Honda CR-X and when she failed to make her manicure appointment at her friend Terry Davis' salon, and then failed to make a 7:00 p.m. pizza date with other friends, she was reported missing. That same day, Marlow and Coffman were at the Redlands Mall visiting his sister Koppers who worked at a restaurant and were supposed to pick her up from work; however, Marlow gave his sister back her keys, telling her that they already had a ride. Coffman, clad in a dress, and Marlow, in a suit and tie, probably seemed rather innocuous to Novis when they asked her for a ride. Earlier that day Marlow had told Coffman that they needed to "get a girl" but Coffman alleged that she did not know that Marlow intended to kill her.

At approximately 7:30 p.m., they took Novis to Marlow's friend Richard Drinkhouse's house who was home alone recovering from a motorcycle accident at the time. Coffman took their hostage into the bedroom after telling Drinkhouse they needed to use the bathroom. Marlow told Drinkhouse that Coffman was trying to get her ATM pin number so they could "rob" her bank account. Drinkhouse didn't appreciate their intrusion into his house to which Marlow assured Drinkhouse that that there wouldn't be any witnesses because how could Novis talk to anyone "if she's under a pile of rocks"? Soon thereafter, Marlow's sister Koppers showed up and she and Coffman left the house to go to a nearby 7-Eleven while Marlow cautioned Drinkhouse not to leave and then returned to the bedroom where Novis was. After Coffman returned, she went into the bedroom to change clothes and after what sounded like the shower running the three of them emerged from the bedroom—Novis' and Marlow's hair were wet (Coffman testified that she had nothing to do with "what went on in the shower"). Novis was handcuffed and had duct tape over her mouth. They left the house and Drinkhouse testified that he never saw Novis again.

The next day, Marlow and Coffman asked Drinkhouse if he wanted to buy an answering machine. Novis' employer Jean Cramer, went to check on her the morning of 10 November when she uncharacteristically failed to appear at work and didn't call. She noticed Novis' car was missing, her front door was ajar, and her bedroom was in disarray. There was no evidence of forced entry and Novis' typewriter and answering machine were missing. On 7 November Koppers sold Novis' answering machine to a friend in exchange for a half-gram of methamphetamine who sold it to someone else and the Redlands Police Department ultimately recovered it. The next day, Harold Brigham who owned the Sierra Jewelry and Loan in Fontana testified that Coffman pawned Novis' typewriter using the victim's identification.

Back at the Robbeloths' house Coffman said Marlow changed clothes and tried to access money from Novis' account at a local First Interstate Bank; however, the PIN number she gave them was incorrect. The following day they ransacked Novis' apartment, found her PIN number, stole her money, pawned the typewriter they stole, disposed of Novis' belongings and then returned to Drinkhouse's house. On 12 November Marlow found out that his sister was in police custody and he and Coffman drove to Big Bear to get rid of Novis' car. They checked into the Bavarian Lodge using a credit card from another victim, Lynell Murray. They abandoned Novis' car on a dirt road south of Santa's Village which was approximately a quarter mile off of Highway 18 in the area. Coffman's fingerprints were found on the license plate, hood, and ashtray while Marlow's prints were found on the hood. The two then proceeded to walk along Big Bear Boulevard clad only in bathing suits despite the chilly weather; the stolen clothes that they had been wearing were discarded along with the handcuffs used on Novis. Receipts for clothing purchased by Marlow and Coffman were found in the clothing's pockets. The .22 caliber pistol the couple owned was in Coffman's purse.

Novis' body was discovered on 15 November lying face down in a shallow grave at a Fontana vineyard. She had been strangled and sodomized.

Dr. Gregory Reiber performed Novis' autopsy on 17 November and conclude that time of death was between five and ten days prior. Evidence of marks on her neck, injuries to her neck muscles, and thyroid cartilage fracture suggested death by strangulation; however, the presence of dirt in her throat also suggested possible suffocation. There was also biological evidence of sodomy.

Lynell Murray

On 12 November, 19-year old psychology student and Prime Cleaners dry cleaning shop clerk Lynell Murray failed to keep a date with her boyfriend, Robert Whitecotton, in Orange County. After noticing that the cleaners looked as though it had been burglarized and ransacked and that Murray's car was parked in the parking lot out back he called the police.

Murray had no idea that the previous day Marlow and Coffman saw her leaving work and that Marlow had commented that she would be "a good one to rob." The following evening at approximately 6:00

p.m., shortly before Murray was to leave work, one Lynda Schafer entered the cleaners and dropped of some clothes with Murray. Schafer would later testify that she saw Coffman "passionately embracing a man", later identified as Marlow, in an alley behind the cleaners.

At 6:30 p.m. that evening Coffman approached Linda Whitlake who was leaving her gym and asked for a ride to her motel, claiming that her car wouldn't start. After Whitlake noticed Marlow in Novis' white car with its hood up she changed her mind about giving them a ride. Coffman said that her boyfriend had decided to call the auto club instead and Whitlake left.

At 7:13 p.m. Coffman checked into room 307 of the Huntington Beach Inn under the name Lynell Murray and used Murray's credit card. At 8:19 p.m. a Bank of America branch in Corona del Mar recorded a balance inquiry into Murray's account and a subsequent withdrawal of $80 occurred, shortly followed by a $60 withdrawal, which left a balance of $4.41. Later that evening Coffman checked into the Compri Hotel in Ontario, California, with Murray's credit card. At midnight Marlow and Coffman ate dinner at the Denny's restaurant across from the hotel, which they paid for with Murray's credit card.

Murray's body would be discovered the following day at approximately 3:00 p.m. in room 307 at the Huntington Beach Inn. Her head was in the bathtub in six inches of water with it and her face bound with strips of towel. She was gagged. Her right arm was secured to her waist with a towel. Her right leg was atop the toilet and her left leg was on the floor. Her ankles looked to have been bound with duct tape as residue was evident. Her bra, nylons, and one earring were missing and she looked to have been raped and urinated on. She had also suffered pre-mortem blunt force trauma to the head, torso injuries, two black eyes, and leg bruising which were consistent with being beaten. The cause of death was determined to be ligature strangulation.

Police finally turned their attention to Marlow and Coffman after finding Novis' driver's license and checkbook in a Taco Bell takeout bag near a dumpster in Laguna Niguel along with papers with both Marlow's and Coffman's names on them. Marlow had attempted to dispose of this damning evidence but missed the dumpster. A statewide alert was issued for both Marlow and Coffman.

Arrest

On 14 November, police were dispatched to a Big Bear, California, mountain lodge after being alerted that Murray's credit card was being used to purchase clothes at a local sporting goods store. The owner of the lodge identified Marlow and Coffman as his latest guests. After finding the lodge empty, the 100-man posse discovered the suspects walking along a mountain road at approximately 3:00 p.m. They surrendered without incident, clad in clothing they had stolen from the dry cleaning shop where Murray had worked. A few hours later Coffman led police to Novis' body. One of the victim's earrings, a .22 caliber pistol and ammunition, credit card receipts with Murray's forged signature, and a Prime Cleaners paper bag with coins were found in Coffman's purse.

The Trial

Nearly three years later Marlow and Coffman would stand trial which commenced on 18 July 1989 in San Bernardino County. At several points throughout the proceedings motions for severance filed by both defendants were denied.

Among the overwhelming evidence were both defendants' fingerprints in Novis' car and that, as previously mentioned, Coffman was linked to the Fontana pawn shop where Novis' typewriter was pawned. In room 307 of the Huntington Beach Inn where Lynell Murray's body was found, a footprint on a bathmat by her body was consistent with Marlow's boots. The aforementioned Taco Bell bag with Novis' license and checkbook and documentation with Coffman's and Marlow's names was recovered. Credit card activity demonstrated where and when the defendants had used Murray's credit card. Additionally, the discarded suit jacket that Marlow had worn when they abducted Novis was found at the Bavarian Lodge and contained identification bearing Marlow's name, various single earrings presumed to be trophies from the murders, a blue ladies wallet, and the handcuffs used on Novis. Novis' vehicle was found near Santa's Village with license plates stolen from a vehicle that was at the Huntington Beach Inn and in a nearby trash can a maintenance worker found a pillowcase containing Murray's bra and laundry receipts from the cleaners where Murray had worked.

Coffman took the stand in her own behalf, painting Marlow to be an abusive man who was violent toward her and threatened both her and her son. She alleged that any violence directed toward the victims were perpetrated by Marlow. With respect to Novis, Coffman testified that on the night of Novis' death, she had dropped Novis and Marlow off at the vineyard and was told to go purchase methamphetamines. Coffman alleges that she drove a short distance, stopped and smoked a cigarette, and then returned to "the sound of digging." Marlow returned to the vehicle alone, threw some items in the back of the car, and then started to beat her for driving away.

Coffman's attorney presented numerous witnesses who corroborated Coffman's allegations of Marlow's violence including Katherine Davis, one of Marlow's ex-wives, and her mother Marlene Boggs; Coffman's former employers in Arizona; Coffman's mother Carol Maender; and clinical psychologist Craig Rath who claimed that Coffman's relationship with Marlow was "precipitated by impaired bonding in her early life", that she was not malingering, and that she did not suffer from antisocial personality disorder.

In Marlow's defense, his sister Veronica Koppers testified about the abuse and neglect the two suffered at the hands of their mother and her father Wendell Hill; about how her father shot her mother and her mother stabbed her father seven times which prompted Doris to move to California in 1963; about visiting her mother at the Sybil Brand Institute for Women and the Frontera State Prison; about how Doris introduced her daughter to drugs much like she did with Marlow and taught her how to burglarize houses; and about the myriad drinking and drug parties hosted at their house. Several witnesses at the trial testified that Doris rarely even mentioned that she had children and paid them little attention when they were together. Despite Marlow claiming responsibility for the murder in Kentucky as well as Novis' and Murray's in California he tried to shift the majority of blame onto Coffman much as she attempted to do to him.

Throughout the trial, Coffman's legal team tried to utilize the "Patty Hearst" defense that she was brainwashed, starved, and the victim of battered women's syndrome who was subjected to frequent physical, emotional, and mental abuse. Once, she claimed, Marlow beat her with a motorcycle clutch plate bruising her face and another time kicked her with his steel-toed boots. She stated that she feared for both her life and that of her then-six-year old son. Coffman's side even presented an expert on battered women's syndrome; however, the jury apparently rejected such claims.

Other testimony suggested that Coffman was the true ringleader and cold, calculated murderess, being far more intelligent than Marlow who would do anything to keep her. At one point, prosecutor Robert Gannon asked Coffman whether her relationship with Marlow was more important than the lives of Corinna Novis and Lynell Murray to which she replied, "Yes."

Sentencing

Both defendants were convicted of the kidnapping, robbery, kidnapping for robbery, residential burglary, forcible sodomy, and murder of Novis and subsequently sentenced to death on 30 August 1989. Coffman became the first women sentenced to death in California since the state reinstated capital punishment in 1977; however, California's reputation as an overly liberal state makes it unlikely that Coffman will ever be put to death.

On 8 March 1992 Marlow received a second death sentence for Murray's murder while Coffman received a life without the possibility of parole sentence added to her death sentence, the former rather moot.

On 19 August 2004 the California Supreme Court unanimously upheld both Marlow's and Coffman's death sentences.

Post-conviction

There continues to be speculation as to whether Coffman controlled or was controlled by Marlow. In fact, while on Death Row, Marlow wrote *I Wish You Were Never Born*, a novel detailing Coffman's and his murderous spree (proceeds of the sale of his book are donated to help abused children). He asserts that their story in the popular media—including an episode of *Wicked Attractions*—was sensationalized and he wanted the truth to be known.

HUSBAND KILLER : THE TRUE STORY OF LARISSA SCHUSTER

ERIN EDWARDS

Larissa Leann Foreman was born January 1, 1960. She grew up on a farm near Clarence Missouri. By all accounts she had a happy childhood. She won first place at the Randolph pony show, her father, Charles, won first place in the men's division and Deeann, her mom, won second in the bareback for pleasure division. Her parents seemed to be very involved in her life. She excelled academically; she was athletic and went after what she wanted with everything she had. She was described as a 'go getter'.

Larissa graduated High school and went on to the University of Missouri Columbia to become a biochemist. She didn't come from a rich family so she would work as a nursing aide at Boone Hospital Center in Columbia Missouri. It's not known whether she liked her work as an aide, however she did like a nurse named Tim Schuster, and he liked her as well. She was electrifying and intoxicating, Tim was enthralled. They started dating after becoming friends and just hanging out together after work.

Finally, in 1982 Tim popped the question, and Larissa said yes. Between 1982 and the birth of their second child Tyler in 1990 there was a whirlwind of things happening. There was the wedding in '82, the birth of their first child, Kristin, and a move to sunny central California, Fresno to be exact.

In the beginning Tim managed the cardiology Department for St Agnes Medical Center. While Larissa worked for Pan Agricultural Laboratories. Larissa saw the company declining and thought it a good time to start her own company; Central California Research Lab. She was ambitious and worked long hours to make her company a success. Tim continued to work at St Agnes and be both Mom and Dad to their two children.

According to friends Bob and Mary Solis, Tim was the one who made sure doctor appointments were kept, homework was done and dinner was cooked and on the table. Larissa ruled her house and Tim having a non-confrontational personality went along with her, if for no other reason than to keep the peace. By this time she was making more than twice what Tim made. It was her money that made it possible for them to move to Clovis and buy a much larger home than the one they had in Fresno. It looked like they had it all...but did they?

By this time Kristen was a teenager and as with most teens there was attitude. Kristen fought with her mother at almost every turn. She stood up to Larissa in such a way that she felt she had no other option than to send her daughter to her parents in Clarence, Missouri. Tim was upset that his wife didn't even discuss this move with him; she'd decided this IS what will happen. And soon his beloved little girl was gone. But still Tim kept quiet.

The Schuster's entered into a bitter, rancorous separation in 2002, after nearly 20 years of marriage and two children. They tried living in the same house after the separation. However Larissa was not happy with this arrangement. From the very beginning she didn't want Tim to have anything to do with Tyler, no visitation and no kind of a relationship with his son at all. This was not okay with Tim. On more than one occasion she made the statement that she wished Tim would just die.

In late June or early July Larissa took Tyler and went on a trip out of state. Tim took this opportunity to secure a condo and move out of the family's home. Larissa was livid that he would have the nerve to leave while she was away and accused him of taking things from the house that didn't belong to him. What earlier seemed like idle threats became something more, she told a neighbor that she should just get it over with and kill Tim herself.

A Plan started formulating shortly after Tim moved out of the Clovis family home. Larissa asked James Fagone a lab assistant and Larissa's sometimes babysitter, sometimes whipping boy if he would help break in to Tim's house and help her get back something he took when he moved out. She felt he wasn't entitled to them and left messages on his answering machine telling him he'd better bring them back...or else.

After returning from a trip Tim came home to a house that had been burglarized and ransacked. One of the things missing...the very set of mixing bowls Larissa had had such a fit over. Who was her accomplice in the break-in...none other than James Fagone? Larissa wasn't shy about what they had done, she told her manicurist Terri Lopez, that after the break-in she would go back to Tim's house and sit in a chair and look around at what they had done. She also told Tami Belshay that "it gave her a feeling that was better than sex."

After the burglary the Schuster's relationship went even further downhill. Tim knew who had broken into his condo. Larissa's bitterness not only let her destroy things in the condo, but she even bragged about keying his truck. She said it made her happy every time she saw the marks on his truck. Tim seemed worried about what his estranged wife was capable of. He moved again, this time to a house in Clovis that had motion sensors and an alarm. He obtained a handgun and a permit to carry a concealed weapon. Larissa had told her manicurist Ms. Lopez that she prayed every night that Tim would just die. At one point Larissa told her that she could kill Tim and get away with it. She also asked one of the employees at CCRL if her boyfriend knew anyone that would kill Tim or at least rough him up. She'd made remarks like this before and all who heard them thought she was just venting because the divorce wasn't going the way she wanted it to. She said she would do anything to keep Tim from getting the business.

According to Bob and Mary Solis, Larissa would belittle and embarrass Tim in front friends and family alike. She seemed to relish the power she had over him.

In late June St Agnes let everyone know that there would be a round of layoffs coming and to be expecting it. Tim and his friend Mary Solis was on the short list to be let go. Larissa laughed when she heard the news. On July 9th Tim, Mary, her husband Bob and another friend Victor Uribe all had dinner together. The group broke up about 10pm that night, before Tim left the Solis' they had made arrangements to meet for breakfast the next morning. Tim never showed for his exit meeting or for breakfast. This worried Bob and Mary, it seems Tim was never late for anything, and if he thought he was going to be late he called. He was also supposed to pick up Tyler that evening.

His friends tried to reach Tim, calling his cell phone. Finally they called Uribe and told him that they couldn't reach Tim and would he go by the house and check on their friend. Uribe arrived at Tim's house and went inside. There didn't seem to be anything out of place, until he went to the bedroom. Tim's watch, wallet and cell phone were lying on the dresser. Uribe was now worried as well. Victor said "He never went anywhere without his cell, he kept it with him at all times, in case the kids needed him."

No one knew what had happened to Tim. The police refused to even take a missing person's report until he'd been missing 24 hours. July 10th when Tim had not been heard from in the allotted time Bob Solis filed the missing person's report. Officer John Willow from the Clovis Police Department responded to the call.

Willow found Tim's handgun under a cushion of a chair. He found Tim's cell phone in the bedroom and called all the numbers in his contacts to see if any of them had seen or heard from Mr. Schuster. When he called Larissa she said she hadn't heard from him either. He also talked to Terri Lopez and she relayed to Willow that the Schuster's were going through a rather nasty divorce. John Willow decided to turn the case over to Detectives Larry Kirkhart and Vincent Weibert.

When they entered Tim's home they noted some damage on the wall behind the chair where the gun was found earlier. They found a briefcase in the same room as the chair. Inside they found a microcassette recorder and tape. In the bedroom they found an answering machine that showed only one number, a cell phone number belonging to Larissa Schuster. Detective Kirkhart then asked Larissa to come to the police station for a chat about her missing husband.

During her interview with the detectives she told them that she and Tim were getting a divorce and that they did not communicate very well with each other. They asked her about her cell number being on the caller ID. She fabricated a story about being asleep on her couch and waking up to find she had pushed some buttons and maybe she had speed dialed Tim. They asked her if she had her phone with her and she said no. Kirkhart called for a pause in the interview and went to the parking lot to find Larissa's car. He looked in the window and saw a phone on the center console, dialed her number and the phone in the car rang.

Kirkhart went back to the interview room and asked Larissa to come with them to unlock her car and retrieve her phone. Back inside the station the interview resumed. The detective went through her contacts that she had on speed dial, none of them were Tim's number.

Larissa's whole demeanor changed, she was shaking and in the opinion of the detectives showing signs of deceit. She came clean and admitted that she had lied to the detectives and she knew she shouldn't have. She claimed she wasn't trying to be deceitful. None the less they let Schuster go home, for now. At this point in their investigation they still had no idea what had happened to Tim. Kirkhart had asked Larissa if she thought that Tim could just cash out some money and leave town, go camping or to Vegas to just get away. She told them she didn't think he would do that, that he wouldn't leave his son like that. This was still just a missing person case and most of Tim's friends thought that perhaps he had just had enough, the divorce, the custody battle, losing his job was to much for him to handle. Tami Belshay, Bob and Mary Solis and Victor Uribe were among those friends. The detectives were thinking the same thing at this point.

With no solid leads on Tim's whereabouts detectives Weibert and Kirkhart kept searching for some clue, however small that might give them some direction on finding Tim. Kirkhart was going through Tim's ledger provided to them by Larissa. And they came across a name they were familiar with…James Fagone. They knew his name because he was the one suspected of breaking into Tim's house with Larissa shortly after Tim moved out of the family home a year earlier. They also knew that he was an associate of sorts of Larissa's.

The following Monday Detectives Kirkhart and Daly called Fagone to come and talk with them. Vince Weibert thought that perhaps Fagone might have some "inside" information on Tim's disappearance.

It seems that Fagone was a babysitter for the Schuster's son Tyler, before and after their separation. James was a good kid according to his attorney Peter Jones. "He's an above average student, higher than a 4.0 grade point average…a gentle spirit."

Fagone was nervous during the police interview. He admitted that Larissa had him help her break into Tim's house and take back things that she didn't want him to have.

James told the detectives that Larissa was going around the house looking for things and he just wanted to get the TV and some other stuff so he wasn't paying attention to what she was doing. Obviously James was scared out of his mind by now, but they pressed him more telling him they "knew he was involved somehow" with Tim's disappearance. Fagone's determination not to tell what had happened, what him and Larissa Schuster had done crumbled.

Fagone confessed that he had been there the night that Tim went missing, that he had gone to his house with a weapon. James relayed to them that Larissa had paid him the $2000 to purchase a stun gun and that he could just keep the rest for himself.

So as the day wore on James conveyed the sordid details of the night in questions.

On the night that Tim lost his job at St Agnes and had dinner with a group of friends, James had done what he was told to do by

Larissa, buy a stun gun. Later he would get the call from her (Larissa). She picked him up and went to Tim's house. James laid in wait in the darkness just outside of his door. He could hear Larissa on the phone telling Tim that Tyler wasn't feeling well and she needed him to come to the front door.

A few moments later Tim opened the front door and James sprung from the shadows and attacked him wrestling him to the ground. Tim was struggling; James was using the stun gun on him, on the arm at first, not sure where else he might have zapped him. Soon Tim stopped struggling and when James looked up he saw Larissa with a rag that had been soaked in chloroform.

Were the detectives hearing this right? Was Fagone confessing to the murder of Timothy Schuster? But if they were going to believe any of it they needed some kind of evidence. They asked about the stun gun again, and what had Fagone done with it. He told them he threw it in a portable toilet on the edge of town. The investigators found the stun gun, right where James told them it should be.

Now at the same time Fagone was being interviewed Clovis Police Department got a call from a woman saying that her boss ask her to do something that in retrospect seemed a little off, suspicious even. Her Boss...Larissa Schuster. Leslie Dodd had been instructed to rent a moving truck by her boss. She was told to use her personal credit card and rent it in her own name not her boss's. A year earlier Larissa had asked the same employee to rent a storage unit near Schuster's lab, again to do it in the employees name and with her personal credit card.

Jim Koch got the call to check it out. He went to the storage unit and walked down the hall. He had been told to look for a blue barrel. When he found Schuster's unit and opened the door "there was a very very strong odor." Koch said. "I had on a breathing apparatus and gloves."

He saw the blue barrel, he opened it.

Koch said in an interview, "And when I opened the barrel I—I saw something that was very, very shocking to me and I recognized immediately as human remains. There was a barrel that's over 3/4 of the way full of fluid and portions of—of—body protruding from the fluid. And the body was obviously decaying. It was placed in acid. And the acid was basically eating away at the body."

Had Larissa Schuster killed her husband and put him in the barrel? According to James Fagone, yes she had, and he had helped her and then watched as she poured a caustic solution in on top of Tim. Worst of all, Tim was probably still alive when the acid was poured on him and he was sealed inside the barrel.

Tim had been found, the truth had come out and the Clovis detectives were on their way to Missouri to arrest Larissa for the murder of her husband Tim. They met her at the airport where she had gone to see her family. According to the detectives that arrested her for the murder she didn't even ask what had happened to Tim or how he died.

Both James Fagone and Larissa Schuster were arrested and charged with 1st degree murder.

Now that the perpetrators of Tim Schuster's murder had been arrested it was time to take them to trial. The murder was committed in the early morning hours of July 10, 2003. There was a lot left to do before the trial could begin.

The Clovis police department had to finish gathering evidence, talk to friends and family to make sure that everything was done correctly. They wanted to make sure that Larissa and James would not be let go on a technicality.

The judge had to decide if he would make this a death penalty case or a life in prison without parole case. That would be decided later. The prosecutor had to prepare a rock solid case and present the evidence to a jury in a manner that would guarantee a conviction. The defense would also be talking to people on behalf of their clients. Find people that had nothing but good things to say about them in hopes of offsetting the horrible truths that would come out at trial.

The judge separated the cases and James and Larissa would be tried separately. James was tried first. His attorney portrayed James as a misguided man who hero worshipped Larissa.

He was found guilty and is now serving a life without parole sentence.

There was so much media coverage on Larissa that the defense asked and received a change of venue. Her trial was moved to Los Angeles.

Monday October 22, 2007 Larissa's trial started. Prosecutor Dennis Peterson relayed to the jury of 9 women and 3 men just how the murder went down. He told them that Tim was still alive when the acid was poured over him while he laid head first inside the blue barrel. Her motive? She didn't want to share anything that they built during their 19 ½ years of marriage. She felt Tim didn't deserve any part of the business, or home and didn't want him to have contact with their tween son, Tyler.

CCRL employees would also testify to the facts of the blue barrel being at the lab and the day Tim was reported missing went to look for it and it was gone. They also said that Larissa had said that she should just shove Tim in the barrel and get rid of him.

A large amount of Hydrochloric acid, 12 gallons and Sulfuric acid, 4 gallons was ordered for Schuster's lab, more than ever before. Leslie Dodd (nee Fichera) testified that, "that was more acid than the lab would use in a year."

Joseph Boatwright thought Larissa was joking when she asked "if he thought a body would fit in the blue barrel."

Juror's watched several hours of Larissa's police interview. She made Tim out to be controlling and having a volatile temper. After seeing that part of the interview Bob Solis testified to the contrary, that Tim was very calm and a non-violent, non-confrontational person.

In another part of the interview with Clovis Detectives Schuster stated that "she prayed that Tim would get over this hostility about the divorce." Her manicurist Terri Lopez told a different story. Lopez said that "she told me she prayed every night he would die."

A hair stylist Becky Holland sometimes did Larissa's hair. During those appointments Larissa would rant about Tim. Holland didn't think much about it because she knew they were going through a divorce. Later though she said the hateful remarks escalated, Holland told the court, "this is getting a little creepy. It was so intense."

The jurors got to hear just how intense it was when they got to hear message after message of Larissa calling her husband awful names and making threats about their children. The prosecutor used these recordings to make a point to the jury; Larissa was in a "murderous rage". Nuttall interjected that these messages were left on Tim's machine 7 months before the murder.

And with this the prosecution rested, hoping that they had proved their case. There was one witness that they really needed to be able to lockdown the case against Schuster, they needed James Fagone. The judge had barred his confession so the jury would never hear in his own words what happened July 10, 2003. But he refused to cooperate with Peterson because he had already filed his appeal. The only thing that might have helped Peterson is the fact that James Fagone had already been convicted of Tim's murder.

Nuttall began the defense's case by telling the jury that neither he nor his client could tell them what had happened to Tim because "we don't know". And since the jury heard nearly nothing about Fagone, Roger Nuttall blamed the murder on him. After all Fagone had already been found guilty of the murder Larissa was now on trial for. Nuttall said in his opening statements that "Tim was an angry man who belittled Larissa in over-compensation for his own failings as a husband and father." And that "he began stalking Larissa after the divorce proceedings started."

Now Defense attorney Nuttall brought in a stream of witnesses that would steer the blame away from his client.

He had a medical expert that said the victim's body was cut in half and that the police had completely missed a second crime scene and the evidence from there would have proved that Fagone and others were responsible for Tim's murder not Larissa.

Nuttall even had psychiatrist Stephen Estner on the stand. Estner said that, "My impression was that Mrs. Schuster was a very direct and assertive person, and Mr. Schuster was a more passive and nurturing personality. And I think they started butting heads over that."

Larissa Schuster took the stand in her own defense and adamantly denied the charges saying, "No, I did not kill my husband." Again James Fagone would have the whole murder put squarely on him. Schuster told the jury, ""I heard him say something like 'there had been an accident and Tim is dead.' I thought he was joking."

She said that the $2000 payment to Fagone was for babysitting Tyler and housesitting while she was away on vacation with her son. Schuster said the large amount of acid was for cleaning a large scale of lab glass. Schuster seemed to explain everything away poking holes in the prosecutor's case. Would it be enough to get an acquittal? Had she actually swayed the jury?

It seemed that the trial was plagued with problems, including accusations of juror misconduct. At least one juror was replaced by an alternate due to disruptive behavior. Another admonished for giving Larissa a 'thumbs up' after her testimony. And yet with all of that...it was time for the jury to deliberate of the weeks of testimony they'd heard.

It took a little more than two days for the jury to decide on a verdict.

Guilty of Murder with a special circumstance of financial gain. The verdict came exactly one year after Fagone's.

Roger Nuttall slowed the sentencing of Larissa Schuster while he tried to find reasons to ask for a new trial. He even used the argument that there may have been juror misconduct. Nuttall wanted to talk to the jurors but Ellison said no. Nuttall appealed and the District court of Appeals told Ellison to contact the jurors on Schuster's behalf. All the jurors and alternates refused to speak to her attorney.

So on May 8, 2008, five months after being found guilty of her estranged husband's murder Larissa Leeann Schuster was sentenced to life in prison without the possibility of parole. Judge Ellison also denied her request for a new trial.

At the sentencing a total of seven people stood up to make statements about how they had been affected by the murder of Timothy Allen Schuster.

Kristen, Tim and Larissa's oldest child and only daughter made an emotionally charged statement to and about her mother.

She called her mother a demon for "taking my father away." And told her. "I pray you're continually haunted at night by the sight and sound of my father fighting for his last breathing moments on this earth. I hope you toss and turn and have horrible nightmares visualizing the horrific act of violence you have committed. Maybe later in life I can learn to forgive you, but I doubt it. This is goodbye, not just for now, but forever. This is goodbye as your daughter."

Kristen was so devastated over her father's murder she reached out to a support group murdervictims.com. Several people shared their own experiences of losing a parent at a young age hoping she could find at least a little peace.

ALICIA LOVERA

The life of Alicia Shayne Lovera looked like something out of a soap opera.

Born into poverty, she was ushered into a life of wealth and privilege when her mother married a rich president of a bank. She grew up to be beautiful, popular and spoiled. But she soon find herself in financial ruin when her stepfather committed suicide, leaving the family with nothing.

Her sense of entitlement still intact, she married a struggling math teacher who couldn't resist her charms.

But when the marriage became an inconvenience, she did what all black widows do.

She killed her husband.

This is her story.

EARLY LIFE

Alicia Shayne Good was born in 1966 to teenage parents. Going by her middle name Shayne, her early life wasn't easy as her parents lacked the necessary resources to provide. Her mother would divorce her father. But when Shayne turned seven-years old things to a turn for the better.

"Her mother and she were poor," journalist Jamie Satterfield said. "Her mother met Brent Mills who was a bank president and they married into that family and Brent adopted Shayne."

The change in life circumstance was jarring to the young Shayne. She was instantly given an upgrade in lifestyle as she the world was now her oyster. There were expensive vacations, cars and garish parties.

Her new stepfather, Brent Mills, was a bank executive who treated Alicia and her mother Sandy to all the spoils his job could bring. He was well regarded in the business community and had several contacts.

But Brent had inherited the bank built by his father and lacked his business acumen. He was lenient in granting loans and the bank soon grew insolvent. He was also suspected of using the bank as a money laundering service for drug dealers.

On the surface, Brent told the family that the allegations were all fraudulent. He gave them every assurance that everything would be okay.

Then he killed himself.

"He took a gun to his head and blew his brains out," forensic psychologist Paula Orange said. "That left an indelible image on Shayne's outlook on life."

His suicide would leave the family in financial ruin. The papers would ridicule Mills, giving voice to all of the wild allegations of his mismanagement. The family would be left shamed and with nothing.

The effect was devastating on Shayne. She would go from being the richest girl in the school to being dirt poor.

Again.

Shayne just wanted to get away. She had entertained aspirations of being broadcast anchor, thinking that her beauty and speaking skills would lead to an easy gig. So she decided to move out of state for college. She would attend a university in Missouri where she would meet Kelly Lovera.

They would marry a year later.

The couple would have two children over the next five years despite being the polar opposites temperamentally.

Kelly was cool, calm and wanted a quiet life. He didn't embrace the partying lifestyle that Shayne wanted.

"Theirs was a union that is hard to comprehend," Orange said. "Kelly was not en route to becoming the next bank president. He was a twenty-year old student who was struggling. He wanted to be a math teacher. Shayne wanted to live a hedonistic lifestyle. She wanted to party and spend lavishly. Why they would get married defies explanation."

Bored in Missouri, Shayne would then convince Kelly to move back to her hometown in Tennessee. Kelly would consent to the move.

A RETURN TO POVERTY

The couple would live in Sevierville which was thirteen miles north of her former luxury home in Gatlinburg. But it was light years away in terms of affluence as they were forced to rent out a small, one story townhouse.

The neighborhood they lived in was called "Frog Alley".

"A luxury once experienced becomes a necessity," Orange said. "Shayne had gotten used to living the high life. But married life, particularly one with of a lack of resources, would prove to be difficult for her."

"Frog Alley was a place for the working poor," Satterfield said. "To come back and live there would be extremely embarrassing for her."

Kelly's focus was not on making money. He was working on his master's degree in mathematics while he took a teaching position at Pellissippi College in Knoxville. Shayne would work various odd jobs to help the family make ends meet and was not happy about that.

"She had wild ambitions to become a news anchor," Orange said. "But she didn't do anything to make that happen. She wanted someone else to do all the work for her just like she experienced when her step-father financed her life."

BOREDOM SETS IN

Shayne entertained neighbors for barbecues and poker nights. The problem is, the only people that seemed to come around were other men.

She was thoroughly bored with her marriage and began to have multiple affairs.

"She would flirt with men in full view of the children," Orange said. "Men would come over ostensibly to play cards. She would play 'footsie' with them underneath the poker table. She didn't want to be a mother and got bored with that act. She wanted to party, to be the rich wild girl that she was as a teenager. The idea of staying home with a boring math teacher and two needy children was anathema to her. She wanted a way out."

The affairs would occur in her apartment when Kelly was away. Different men would come and go at various hours.

"He's (Kelly) cramping my style," Shayne told one of her lovers. "And you're so much better than him."

"Thanks," her lover said with a grin.

"Do you know anything about how to poison someone?"

"Excuse me?"

"You know," Shayne said. "How certain poisons are undetectable."

Shayne would test the waters with her lovers. She would ask them about poisons in a joking manner. But then they would soon realize that she was serious. There was an ulterior motive to her affairs.

She wanted to find someone to kill her husband.

And she would find a willing assassin in Brett Rae.

THE NEXT DOOR NEIGHBOR

Brett was young and inexperienced with women. He had never encountered anyone like the sexy Shayne Lovera.

"Brett fell very hard for Shayne," Satterfield said. "Their affair started very quickly. And it was hot and heavy."

"Brett was a rich kid," Satterfield said. "His father was a newspaper publisher (Rick Rae, a Canadian publisher of the Sevier County newspaper). He was a well-to-do guy. He was just wild. He was just one of those people who was 'full-on' all of the time. He was up for anything."

And he was completely infatuated with Shayne.

Shayne set up Brett the same way she set up her other lovers. After a torrid session of lovemaking, she popped the question.

Will you kill my husband?

"I'll do anything for you," he told her with baited breath.

Shayne offered him a deal.

"If he were to get rid of Kelly," Satterfield said. "Then he would get her. That's what Brett wanted."

"Brett let his little head do the thinking for his big head," Orange said. "He was going to inherit money from his father so he had absolutely nothing to gain by killing Shayne's husband. Nothing except sex which of course if he had money, he would have more options than a narcissistic married woman. He simply did not have the life experience to see Shayne for what she was."

She would have a party on November 5th, 1994, an outdoor barbecue with gambling and drinking. Kelly left the party early and went to sleep on the couch.

Brett would be the last one to leave that evening. On his way out the door, they both noticed Kelly asleep on the couch.

"It was a spontaneous thing," Orange said. "They didn't have a murder weapon so they used whatever was immediately available. That would be the baseball bat of Kelly's son."

Kelly would then be bludgeoned to death.

"The plan was to put him in his own vehicle," Satterfield said. "And make it look like an accident."

Brett then dragged Kelly into his jeep and drove down Highway 14. He parked near an embankment and pushed the jeep down the side, watching it carom into a tree.

He then called one of his friends to pick him up.

Brett did not keep the news of the murder to himself. He would brag to two of his friends of what he had done.

"I put him (Kelly) over a hundred foot embankment," Brett said. "I fucked his wife and killed his ass. She told me I'd get more sex and more money if I get rid of him so I did."

Brett told his friends of the other methods he thought of using to kill Kelly but that he decided to beat him to death with the baseball bat then "stage a car crash."

FINDING THE BODY

A pair of tourists would discover Kelly's black jeep below the road. Inside, they would see his bloodied dead body. Initially, they believed that he was the victim of an accident. They called the authorities and reported that it appeared as if his jeep had gone off the road and hit a tree

Park Ranger Jerry Grubb was notified of the "accident" at the Great Smoky Mountains National Park.

The whole scene, however, looked suspicious from the get-go.

"Just wasn't any skid marks," Grubb said. "No disturbed gravel. There just wasn't any disturbance in that area."

Grubb looked inside the jeep and found the body of Kelly Lovera, laying in a pool of blood trailing toward the front seat. The blood should have been trailing behind the victim if he had, in fact, struck the tree head on.

Additionally, Kelly's injuries were not consistent with a car crash victim. The facial injuries appeared to be the result of a beating, not the impact of the jeep against the tree.

MURDER ON THEIR HANDS

The autopsy would reveal that Kelly had been beaten to death and a homicide investigation ensued. Authorities would then visit Shayne's apartment and inform her of her husband's death.

She would go into hysterics, sobbing uncontrollably.

"Do you know why anyone would want to do this to him?" an investigator asked.

"He doesn't have any enemies!" she bawled.

But an officer would notice blood splatter on the glass of Kelly's diploma that was placed on a wall near the couch. They would obtain a search warrant and a crime team would arrive, spraying luminol over the apartment.

Luminol lightens up blood stains when a fluorescent ray is scanned over it.

"The whole living room lit up like a Christmas tree," Orange said. "That is when they knew they had the guilty party."

Detectives then began to question neighbors who all pointed their fingers at Brett Rae, the lover of Shayne.

Both Shayne and Brett were arrested and charged with first-degree premeditated murder.

Brett would confess quickly. He admitted to using the baseball bat and then staging the car wreck. He would be represented by Robert Ritchie who would prep him for the murder trial for nearly three months. Ritchie, however, would notice that Brett was completely obsessed with Shayne. He then turned the case over to Robert Ogle but two weeks before the trial Alan Feltes was brought in as Brett was given joint representation.

"His attorneys were flabbergasted at his refusal to give up Shayne," Orange said. "He was truly in love with her and wanted to protect her even if it meant incriminating himself."

"I did it," Brett insisted. "Just leave her out of it."

Feltes told Brett that there was no way he could win the case with all of the evidence stacked against him. The only thing Brett cared about was putting Shayne in jeopardy.

THE TRIAL

Park Ranger Jerry Grubb would testify against the killing duo, presenting the forensic evidence found at the home and jeep. Friends and family would testify that both Shayne and Brett had bragged to them about what they had done.

Going in desperation mode, Shayne would then take the stand. She wanted to tell her version of what happened that night.

"Brett had stopped by to talk to me when Kelly came out and confronted him," Shayne said. "They began fighting and Brett picked up a baseball bat. He swung it only to keep Kelly away. But then he accidentally hit him and killed him."

Shayne would go on to say that she didn't witness any of this. She was asleep and really knew nothing that happened.

"Brett and I were not lovers," Shayne said. "We were nothing more than neighbors. It was a case of fatal attraction. He had a thing for me and wanted to kill my husband."

She didn't know, however, that when both she and Brett were released on bail they were followed by a Siever County Sheriff. He followed them into the mountains and saw them having intercourse in the woods.

When Shayne was confronted with this evidence, she tried to regroup.

"I had sex with Brett," Shayne said. "But only because I had to. He threatened to involve me in the murder plot. My purpose in going there was trying to save what little bit of life I had left at that point."

The explanation did not go over well with the jury. It took them only an hour and a half to return with a guilty verdict.

OFF TO JAIL

On January 29th, 1996, both Shayne and Brett would be convicted of Kelly's murder. They would not be given the death penalty, however. The prosecution wanted a sentence of life without parole.

Feltes approached by the attorneys for Shayne. They stated that a plea agreement would be possible but it would have to be a package deal with Brett.

Feltes advised Brett to take the deal as the plea agreement would guarantee him a life sentence with possibility of parole. If he didn't take the deal, the odds would be that he would be facing life without parole.

"Just don't do anything to hurt Shayne," Brett said. "I want to see her."

"What?"

"I want to see her before I take the deal."

Brett would persist in wanting to see Shayne. Instead he would take the deal.

"His attorneys described him as having the saddest eyes they had ever seen in a courtroom," Orange said. "He was truly in love with Shayne. She, on the other hand, threw him under the bus. She was willing to say whatever it took to get herself off and it backfired."

THE AFTERMATH

Kelly's children would be placed into the care of his parents. Brett and Shayne would receive life with parole after twenty-five years.

Brett would later try to appeal his sentencing despite agreeing to a plea bargain which barred him from doing so.

His claim would be rejected.

Ray would write that "his trial was ineffective for encouraging him to accept the state's offer of life with possibility of parole; failing to prepare for mitigating circumstances at the sentencing phase; failing to properly conduct a pre-trial investigation; failing to adequately consult with him during critical stages of the proceedings; failing to advise him of his rights to direct appeal and collateral attack of his conviction; deficient performance of counsel at trial; his guilty plea was coerced and involuntary; and his conviction is void as violating the protection against double jeopardy."

"He had conceded his guilt during the guilty plea hearing and that his attorneys did the best they could...he made these admissions only because the attorneys instructed him to do so and although he agreed that he believed himself to be guilty of first degree murder at the time of his plea, he now retracts that admission."

Brett's attorney Feltes would dispute his allegations, stating that he "never had any problem with Brett being incoherent or not understanding anything he was told or advised."

Both Brett and Shayne remain in prison, waiting to be paroled in 2025.

www.ingramcontent.com/pod-product-compliance
Lightning Source LLC
Chambersburg PA
CBHW021210160726
47994CB00001B/422